TOPSY TURVY:

A Book for All in One

Compiled by
J. Michael Mahoney

AuthorHouse™ LLC
1663 Liberty Drive
Bloomington, IN 47403
www.authorhouse.com
Phone: 1-800-839-8640

Published by AuthorHouse 9/15/2014

ISBN: 978-1-4343-7547-6 (sc)
ISBN: 978-1-4343-7831-6 (e)

Library of Congress Control Number: 2008902487

**"Dedicated with love to my three children
and five grandchildren."**

My affection hath an unknown bottom, like the bay of Portugal.
—*Shakespeare,* As You Like It, *IV, I, 219*

Preface

With a clip here and a snip there, Mike Mahoney has managed to gather a most impressive array of quotations, gleaned from books, magazines, and newspapers over many years. In this effort, he has taken time to peer into the lives of those individuals most people might not find interesting or worthy of attention. However, Mike has found nuggets of truth, wisdom, history, humor, passion, and a host of other emotions in even the most innocent words spoken by the famous and the unknown alike.

Susan Goodrich Giffin
August 2008

All proceeds accruing to the author from sales of this book are being donated to the Child Hurbinek Memorial Scholarship Endowment at Princeton University, USA.

See Quotation #657

Mr. Mahoney is also the author of

SCHIZOPHRENIA:
The Bearded Lady Disease

[**www.schizophrenia-thebeardedladydisease.com**]

and the poem

XCIRCUM

[**www.XCIRCUM.com**]

Appreciation

The collector of the quotations in this book owes a profound debt of gratitude to every source whose work he has chosen to include in it. Each one imparts to us all the wisdom, humor, or sadness of that source's lifetime of experience, be it a long life or tragically, as in some cases, a brief one, in the most succinct yet occasionally most powerful and affecting way.

Since this collection was assembled over a period of many years, without any thought of ever having it published, the actual provenance of some of the quotations in it has been lost, forgotten, or never known in the first place. Therefore, to anyone whose quotation(s) appears here without due attribution, sincerest apologies are extended and assurance is hereby given that the unintentional lapse will be corrected immediately upon notification to the publisher of that source's true provenance.

Finally, deep appreciation and thanks is extended to that outstanding freelance editor and writer, Susan Giffin and to Monica Wethmar-Christiaansen, a dedicated, expert editorial facilitator, for taking charge of a notebook filled with a multitude of quotations, collected over a period of some forty-plus years, and typing and arranging them, still in their original "topsy turvy" condition, so that hopefully they can be enjoyed and appreciated by many other passionate quotation lovers.

J.M.M.

Note:

The letters SNN, in TOPSY TURVY: *A Book for All in One,* mean "source not noted."

The letters JMM mean J. Michael Mahoney, the author.

1. **A mind that is stretched to a new idea never returns to its original dimension.**
    —*Oliver Wendell Holmes*

2. **If there is harmony in the house, there is order in the nation. If there is order in the nation, there will be peace in the world.**
    —*Chinese proverb*

3. **In schizophrenia, the victory lies with repression.**
    —*Sigmund Freud*

4. **One of the oldest human needs is having someone to wonder where you are when you don't come home at night.**
    —*Margaret Mead, anthropologist*

5. **We do not remember days; we remember moments.**
    —*Cesare*

6. **Old age clings to my feet like dense pitch.**
    —*Czeslaw Milosz*

7. **A theory is proposed relating schizophrenia to sex-identity alienation in the early years of life.**
    —*David C. McClelland and Norman F. Watt, Journal of Abnormal Psychology, 1968.*

8. **There may be more to learn by climbing the same mountain a hundred times than by climbing a hundred different mountains.**
    —*Richard Nelson, The Island Within*

9. **Hard work is good for the soul. It keeps you from feeling sorry for yourself because you don't have time.**
    —*Minnie Sinclair*

10. **When one is forced to drink black milk from dawn to dusk, whether in the death camps of Nazi Germany, or while lying in a possibly luxurious crib, but there subjected to the unconscious death wishes of what overtly may be a conscientious mother - in either situation, a living soul has death for a master.**
    —*Bruno Bettelheim, SURVIVING – and Other Essays, Alfred A. Knopf, New York, 1979, p. 111.*

11.   **<u>Man found dead on houseboat</u>**
      Sausalito — A man called 911 about 3 PM yesterday to say some-
      one planned to kill himself or herself.
      When police arrived, they found a man who lived on a boat at
      Schoonmaker Marina had shot himself in the head. His name
      was withheld pending notification of the next of kin.
      —Marin Independent Journal, January 27, 1994.

12.   **Only 16 percent of the 853 cultures on record expect a man to**
      have just one wife at a time. But in the vast majority of societies
      in which men are permitted to have several wives at once, only
      5 to 10 percent actually do.
      —SNN

13.   **Everything should be made as simple as possible, but not more**
      so.
      —Albert Einstein

                                          ❊

14.   **All religious cults spring from the repressed homosexual**
      passions of their paranoid schizophrenic founders.
      —JMM

15.   **It's not that I'm so smart. It's just that I stay with problems**
      longer.
      —Albert Einstein

16.   **We do not think of the great open plains, the beautiful rolling**
      hills, and the winding streams with tangled growth, as "wild."
      Only to the white man was nature a "wilderness" and only to
      him was the land "infested" with "wild" animals and "savage"
      people. To us it was tame ... Not until the hairy man from the
      east came and with brutal frenzy heaped injustices upon us and
      the families we loved was it "wild" for us.
      —Chief Luther Standing Bear of the Oglala band of Sioux, early twentieth
      century.

17.   **Do not go where the path may lead. Go instead where there is**
      no path and leave a trail.
      —Ralph Waldo Emerson

18. **Growth is possible only to the extent that one can endure confusion and uncertainty.**
—*Harold Searles, M.D., <u>Schizophrenia and Related Subjects.</u>*

19. **Look, I've told you this before. I was no hero. My great honor was to serve in the company of heroes. I was privileged to observe a thousand acts of courage and compassion and love and that's the great honor of my life. Their approval is my last ambition.**
—*Senator John McCain, as told to Christopher Matthews.*

20. **Two women who are imprisoned together in the same cell for twenty-five years are released on the same day. Before they go their separate ways, they stand together outside the prison gate and talk for an hour.**
—*Old Russian joke.*

21. **I have made no wild promises except one – honest government.**
—*Ernest Johnson, Massachusetts state senator.*

22. **Somebody has to give himself**
as the price of a new frontier.
Somebody has to take a course
and climb to a rendezvous, where a lonesome man with a will to learn can make the truth shine through.
—*Gill Robb Wilson, a founding father of America's Civil Air Patrol.*

23. **Nothing before had ever made me thoroughly realize, though I had read various scientific books, that science consists in grouping facts so that general laws or conclusions may be drawn from them.**
—*<u>The Autobiography of Charles Darwin</u>*

24. **...in its deepest nature, schizophrenia arises from a bisexual conflict, and this bisexual conflict eventually leads to a state where the heterosexual factor is relinquished.**
—*Maurits Katan, M.D., 1954.*

25. **We must recognize that the sexual affections are still the greatest constructive forces of the personality if properly conditioned and adjusted, but also that they may become the most insidiously, irresistibly destructive if perverted or**

unconditionally repressed.
—*Edward J. Kempf, M.D., Psychopathology, C. V. Mosby Company, St. Louis, MO, 1920.*

26.   **I wish I were a man. If I were a man I would be Richard Burton, but, being only a woman, I would be Richard Burton's wife.**
—*Isabel Burton*

27.   **Shut up. I am busy.**
—*Radio operator on the Titanic to warnings from other ships nearby that there were icebergs in the area.*

✳

28.   **It would seem that the schizophrenic patient is often of the third generation of abnormal persons of whom we can gain some information. The preceding two generations of mothers appear to have been obsessive, schizoid women who did not adjust well to men. There is some evidence that they were, in a sense, immature and that within the obsessive character structure could be found hysterical difficulties.**

   It is to be noted, also, that there are two preceding generations of men who are not masters, or equals, in their own marriages and homes, or psychosexually very successful, and who are often described as immature, alcoholic, and passive, or hard-working, self-centered, and detached from the family. We do not know what sort of mothers and fathers these fathers of schizophrenics may have had, but it could be presumed that the fact that they let themselves be married to mothers of schizophrenics implies something concerning their own mothers.

   Loosely, the pattern which emerges is that of two generations of female ancestors who were aggressive, even if in a weak-mannered and tearful way, and two generations of male ancestors who were effeminate, even if the effeminacy was disguised by obsessive or psychopathic tendencies.
—*Lewis B. Hill, M.D., Psychotherapeutic Intervention in Schizophrenia.*

29.   **In his 29th year, Siddhartha Gautama, the Buddha, decided to seek enlightenment but felt he could not achieve it with a family in tow. So the founder of Buddhism left his wife, Yasodhara - the cousin he had married when he was 16 - and their son to**

spend the rest of his life wandering India as a teacher and religious leader.
—*SNN*

30. **You know, I had a drinking problem. Right now, I should be in a bar in Texas, not the Oval Office. There is only one reason that I am in the Oval Office and not in a bar: I found faith. I found God. I am here because of the power of prayer.**
—*George W. Bush, 2003.*

31. **Should it really turn out that Jesus' object world must be considered by the doctor as in some degree the world of a sick man, still this conclusion, regardless of the consequences that follow from it and the shock to many that would result from it must not remain unuttered, since reverence for truth must be exalted above everything else.**
—*Albert Schweitzer, in the preface to the 1913 edition of his book, The Psychiatric Study of Jesus, Exposition and Criticism.*

32. **Rulers who wish to subvert the public liberty may have found an established clergy convenient auxiliaries. A just government, instituted to secure liberty, does not need the clergy... These are the fruits of that legal establishment known as Christianity: pride and indolence in the clergy, ignorance and servility in the laity, and in both clergy and laity, superstition, bigotry, and persecution.**
—*James Madison, co-author of the U.S. Constitution and the Bill of Rights.*

33. **I love my children. But I am not in love with them. I am in love with their father.**
—*Ayelet Waldman, "Modern Love," The New York Times, March 27, 2005.*

34. **Work subjects you to its laws, pares you down, fortifies you, but you remain unchanged. But love ... that certainty that someone awaits you eagerly raises you to a different level of consciousness, indeed to a level greater than life itself.**
—*Henry Bruckau*

35. **The mother's attitude was so subtly ingratiating and yet domineering that she would almost have to be destroyed as a**

mother if the patient were to free herself from its terrible influence and win her own womanhood and independence. [Likewise for male patients – JMM]
—*Edward J. Kempf, M.D., Psychopathology.*

36. **Not infrequently the schizophrenic illness is precipitated in a setting of rejection in a love affair.**
—*Harold Searles, M.D., Schizophrenia and Related Subjects.*

37. **Understanding of another human being can never be complete, but as it grows toward completeness, it becomes love almost inevitably.**
—*Roderick L. Haig-Brown, To Know a River.*

38. **A leader is a dealer in hope.**
—*Napoleon Bonaparte*

39. **Masturbation is the primal addiction.**
—*Sigmund Freud*

40. **We're lost, but we're making good time.**
—*Yogi Berra*

41. **At the Mirage Hotel, he gambled away $20,000 in what was apparently a last minute bid for solvency. He took a handful of sleeping pills, then placed a plastic bag over his head. The police found a handwritten note to Hecht and another informing the hotel's managers that his decision had nothing to do with the quality of their service.**
—*Name of suicide person deleted for privacy reasons.*

42. **When it shall be said in any country in the world, my poor are happy; neither ignorance nor distress is to be found among them; my jails are empty of prisoners, my streets of beggars; the aged are not in want, the taxes are not oppressive; the rational world is my friend, because I am a friend of its happiness – when these things can be said, then may that country boast of its constitution and its government.**
—*Thomas Paine, in Thomas Paine, A Political Life by John Keane.*

43. **The secret of happiness is whores.**
—*Sam Spiegel, movie producer, as told to Harold Pinter.*

44. **How old would you be if you didn't know how old you was?**
    —*Satchel Paige, baseball legend.*

45. **Only the dead have seen the end of war.**
    —*Plato*

46. **You can be a king or a street sweeper, but everybody dances with the Grim Reaper.**
    —*Robert Alton Harris, 39, executed at San Quentin Prison.*

47. **This mixed blessing and burden must be why the astro-physicist Chandrasekhar continued working until his mid-80s, why a visitor to Einstein's apartment in Bern found the young physicist rocking his infant with one hand while doing mathematical calculations with the other. This mixed blessing and burden must have been the "sweet hell" that Walt Whitman referred to when he realized at a young age that he was destined to be a poet. "Never more," he wrote, "shall I escape."**
    —*Alan Lightman*

48. **Our land is more valuable than your money. It will last forever. ...This land will be here to give life to men and animals. We cannot sell the lives of men and animals; therefore, we cannot sell this land... You can count your money and burn it within the nod of a buffalo's head, but only the Great Spirit can count the grains of sand and the blades of grass of these plains. As a present to you, we will give you anything we have that you can take with you; but the land, never.**
    —*A chief of one of the principal bands of northern Blackfeet, upon being asked to sign one of the first treaties in his region.*

49. **It is our conclusion that for most people high levels of erotic arousal tend to generate moderately assaultive tendencies.**
    —*SNN*

50. **The heart has its reasons that reason knows not of.**
    —*Blaise Pascal, seventeenth-century philosopher and mathematician.*

51. **Man can endure earthquake, epidemic, dreadful disease, every form of spiritual torment; but the most dreadful tragedy that can befall him is and will remain the tragedy of the bedroom.**
    —*Leo Tolstoy*

52. **<u>XCIRCUM</u>**

To cut, or not to cut - that is the question:
Whether 'tis nobler in the mind to suffer
The scalpels and razors of outrageous surgeons
Or to take arms against a sea of CIRCUMCISORS
And by opposing end them. To defy, to protest —
No more —and by a protest to say we end
The heartache and the thousand unnatural shocks
That flesh is heir to. 'Tis a consummation
Devoutly to be wished. To defy, to protest —
To protest, perchance to prevail; ay, there's no rub,
For in that protest of defiance the prevailing may come
When we no longer shuffle off this mortal prepuce,
Must give them pause. There's the respect
That makes calamity of violating Nature.
For who would bear the barbarism and atavism of circumcision,
The priest's wrong, the proud doctor's false hygiene,
The pangs of unlubricated love, the law's indifference,
The insolence of ritualism, and the spurns
That patient child endures as the unworthy takes,
When it itself must later better make
With a full bodkin? Who would circumcision bear,
To grunt and sweat over a weary wife,
But that the dread of something worse than death,
The undiscovered castration, from whose bourn
No traveller returns, puzzles the will,
And makes us rather bear those ills we have
Than fly to others that we know not of -
Thus cowardice does make capons of us all,
And thus the native hue of intelligence
Is sicklied o'er with the pale cast of primitivism
And phalli of great pitch and moment
With this regard their currents turn awry
And lose the name of being civilized.
—Soft you now,
The fair n'Ophelia!
—Nymph, in thy embraces
Be all my mutilations remembered.
—*J. Michael Mahoney, with apologies to William Shakespeare.*

53. **Suicide is the ultimate castration. It is most often carried out by those who reject their gender role and wish to be of the opposite sex.**
—*JMM*

54. **Sex is dirty if you do it right.**
—*Mother of a Roman Catholic priest.*

55. **Being born a woman is my awful tragedy. From the moment I was conceived I was doomed to sprout breasts and ovaries rather than penis and scrotum, to have my whole circle of action, thought and feeling rigidly circumscribed.**
—*Sylvia Plath, The Unabridged Journals, 1950-1962, edited by Karen B. Kukil, New York: Anchor Books.*

56. **It is fitting that we pay tribute to Abraham Lincoln, who was born in a log cabin that he built with his own hands.**
—*Dan Flood, congressman from Pennsylvania.*

57. **Earlier Americans held views about children and sexuality that would be disturbing today [1997]. In 1889, the age of female consent was 10 in 14 states, including Alabama and New Jersey, and as young as 7 in Delaware. Campaigns led by early feminists helped raise the age to 18. "In a way, however, innocence then became eroticized," Ms. Coontz said. "Lack of experience, innocence, became the ideal for the marriageable woman. But what is the ultimate lack of experience, if not the pre-pubescent?"**
—*SNN*

58. **We have yet to study the mechanism of homosexuality in women. The inversion of the love interest in men has received more attention. We have, from psychoanalysis, data which trace the origin of the homosexual component to the attachment to the mother, with identification with the father.**
—*Clara Thompson, M.D., Personal Psychopathology.*

59. **I put my face close to the thick glass plate in front of a puff adder in the Zoological Gardens, with the firm determination of not starting back if the snake struck at me; but, as soon as the blow was struck, my resolution went for nothing and I jumped a yard or two backwards with astonishing rapidity. My will and**

reason were powerless against the imagination of a danger which had never been experienced.
—*Charles Darwin, on putting himself to a test of whether willpower can overcome a strong emotional reaction.*

60.   As Lincoln said to prominent political leaders who urged him to back away from the Emancipation Proclamation or face possible defeat for re-election in 1864: "The promise being made, must be kept." The man who had contemplated suicide at the age of thirty-one but drew back because he "had done nothing to make any human being remember that he had lived" eventually caused the whole world to remember that he had.
—*SNN*

61.   Interestingly, Nash's gut instinct — not wanting to be drafted into the army — has since been validated by schizophrenia researchers. None of the life events known to produce mental disorders such as depression or anxiety neurosis — combat, death of a loved one, divorce, loss of a job — have ever been convincingly implicated in the onset of schizophrenia. But several studies have since shown that basic military training during peacetime can precipitate schizophrenia in men with a hitherto unsuspected vulnerability to the illness. Although the study subjects were all carefully screened for mental illnesses, hospitalization rates for schizophrenia turned out to be abnormally high, especially for draftees.   [Homosexual temptation in the close quarters of barrack's life triggers homosexual panic, followed by repression, leading to schizo-phrenic symptomatology. -JMM]
—*Sylvia Nasar, A Beautiful Mind, p. 162.*

62.   Great gams, love yams, mostly honey. Feminine DWF, 35, 5'6" blonde/blue. Seeking S/DWM, who can whistle a tune.
—*A personal ad.*

63.   I know, I know, everyone matters to me. I don't know if that's good or bad. I think it's a blessing and a curse. Don't feed into the dark side. I'm aware that I just can't ignore all the people who display the qualities of malice and hatred I dislike. Some require a watchful eye. This is all for now.
—*Justin Wesley Jones, 19, diary, February 11, 1994, died March 27, 1994. Murdered while going to the aid of a man being robbed.*

64.　**...in them [schizophrenics] the early childhood tie to the parent has never been outgrown.**
　　—Harry Stack Sullivan, M.D., Personal Psychopathology, p. 262.

65.　**The older I get, the better I used to be.**
　　—Sandy Koufax, baseball pitcher.

66.　**Death solves all problems. No man, no problem.**
　　—Josef Stalin

67.　**...the nothingness of the hopes and strivings which chases most men restlessly through life came to my consciousness with considerable vitality. Out yonder there was this huge world, which exists independently of us human beings and which stands before us like a great, eternal riddle, at least partially accessible to our inspections and thinking. The contemplation of this world beckoned like a liberation...**
　　—Albert Einstein, as told to Alan Lightman.

68.　**The return of the repressed.**
　　—Sigmund Freud

69.　**A moment of insight can be worth a lifetime of experience.**
　　—Oliver Wendell Holmes

70.　**Tourist dives into jet engine**
　　Port-of-Spain, Trinidad — An American tourist was killed Sunday after throwing himself into the engine of a taxiing jetliner at Piarco International Airport, police said.
　　Authorities said the death was an apparent suicide.
　　Police said Daniel John O'Brien, 31, of Roselle, IL, near Chicago, scaled an airport wall in the nude, attacked four security guards and stole their four-wheel-drive vehicle.
　　He drove the jeep onto the tarmac to a British Airways 747 that was readying for takeoff. Guards said O'Brien scrambled out of the wrecked jeep, smeared grease on his bleeding shoulder, then ran back to the jetliner and threw himself into the engine.
　　—Newspaper article.

71.　**There is a tincture of homosexuality in everyone.**
　　—Karl A. Menninger

72. **Courage, resignation to the laws of nature, a profound contempt for all superstition, the noble pleasure of feeling oneself to be of a different nature to fools, and the exercise of the faculty of thought are true consolations.**
—Voltaire

73. **Marilyn Monroe is a soldier... The first duty of a soldier is to obey her commander-in-chief.**
—Marilyn Monroe, commenting to her psychotherapist about her affair with John F. Kennedy.

74. **You guys are so unfair.**
—Donita Jo Artis, a twenty-four-year-old Pittsburgh, Pennsylvania mother, to a judge and prosecutor after being denied custody of her three-year-old son and sentenced to two to ten years in prison for beating him until he was blind, deaf, and unable to walk .

75. **Nor must we overlook the probability of the constant inculcation in a belief in God on the minds of children producing so strong and perhaps an inherited effect on their brains not yet fully developed, that it would be as difficult for them to throw off their belief in God, as for a monkey to throw off its instinctive fear and hatred of a snake.**
—Charles Darwin, <u>The Autobiography of Charles Darwin</u>.

76. **No man ever knows what true happiness is until he has a complete set of false teeth and has lost all interest in the opposite sex.**
—Lord Roseberry

77. **There are more things in heaven and earth, Horatio, than are dreamt of in your philosophy.**
—One of Sigmund Freud's favorite quotations, from Shakespeare's <u>Hamlet.</u>

78. **There are more than 10,000 dead in Sarajevo, of whom more than 1,700 were children. So we cannot think that Maja's death was anything special. But of course she was our Maja, so we think it is special.**
—Branko Djokic, father of Maja, killed by Serbian mortar shrapnel during the Bosnian conflict.

79.   **He is ungenerous. He asks but never gives ... never a word of praise for other people.**
      —*Leonard Woolf, on the faults of Lytton Strachey, the author.*

80.   **It takes many minds and hearts to cure a schizophrenic.**
      —*Frieda Fromm-Reichman, M.D.*

81.   **We are all the center of our own little universe.**
      —*SNN*

82.   **The only way to get rid of temptation is to yield to it.**
      —*Oscar Wilde*

83.   **Freud makes an early reference in his *Three Contributions to the Theory of Sex,* in which there is offered the hypothesis that the development of female sexuality contains important variations from that of the male in that the center of interest must shift in the pattern from the clitoris to the vagina - the clitoris and the penis having similar likeness, the vagina being the typically female organ. Further light is shed from later writings on the "castration complex" and "penis envy" in women, and the possibility of problems arising in the female as a result of physiological difference receives attention. In brief, the psychic development of woman must undergo an adjustment similar to that in the physiological realm, if she is to attain adulthood.**
      —*Clara Thompson, M.D., Personal Psychopathology, by Harry Stack Sullivan, M.D..*

84.   **The magic of sex.**
      —*Sigmund Freud*

85.   **If you bring forth what is within you, what you bring forth will save you. If you do not bring forth what is within you, what you do not bring forth will destroy you.**
      —*Jesus, as attributed in the "Gospel of Thomas" [Jesus – the first psychoanalyst – JMM].*

86.   **For years Washington has alternated between putting its head in the sand and saying there is no large number of destitute people in our midst who need food and clothing, and then saying the states should take care of them if there are... The Federal Government has always had and still has a continuing**

responsibility for the broader public welfare. I pledge you, I pledge myself, a New Deal.
—*Franklin D. Roosevelt, July 2, 1932.*

87. **<u>Apparent UCSF Suicide Identified as Student</u>**
A student who apparently jumped to her death from the University of California Medical Center research tower was identified by the medical examiner's office yesterday as 28-year-old Marie-Pierre Laget of San Francisco [male/female name – JMM]
—<u>*San Francisco Chronicle,*</u> *date not noted.*

88. **I ain't got no quarrel with the Vietcong. No Vietcong ever called me nigger.**
—*Muhammad Ali, on refusing to register for the draft during the Vietnam War.*

❀

89. **His mother emerges as a perpetually uneasy woman who was completely and unquestionably self-centered.**
—*SNN*

90. **On this tour I had a striking instance how easy it is to overlook phenomena, however conspicuous, before they have been observed by anyone. We spent many hours in Cwm Idwal, examining all the rocks with extreme care, as Sedgwick was anxious to find fossils in them; but neither of us saw a trace of the wonderful glacial phenomena all around us; we did not notice the plainly scored rocks, the perched boulders, the lateral and terminal moraines. Yet these phenomena are so conspicuous that, as I declared in a paper published many years afterwards in the Philosophical Magazine, a house burnt down by fire did not tell its story more plainly than did this valley. If it had still been filled by a glacier, the phenomena would have been less distinct than they are now.**
—<u>*The Autobiography of Charles Darwin*</u>

91. **The long-nosed Tapir is said to be "insanely ardent."**
—*Newspaper article.*

92. **Get off my train, you little bastard!**
—Man in wedding dress yelling at his dog, overheard at the Old Monterey Farmers' Market by Lulu Drake, (<u>San Francisco Chronicle</u>, Courtesy of Leah Garchik, July 5, 2006).

93. **The snake pit of the title referred to is the medieval practice of lowering the mentally ill into snake pits in the belief that a fright that would unhinge a sane person would cure an insane one.**
—Newspaper book review.

94. **I could no more stop reading his biography than I could stop reading Saul Bellow after he blew the blinds off the windows in my head.**
—John Leonard

95. <u>**Death of a King**</u>
Researching the death of King Kalakaua of Hawaii in 1891, writer Oakley Hall found a log to toss onto the fire of debate about the responsibility of the press to report on intimate details of a statesman's life.

A *Chronicle* report of the King's death was straightforward and dignified. The *Examiner* described the scene at the bedside:

Next to a clergyman who prayed over the king "leaned Kalaua, the young Kauaka girl who has attended the King since she was a child. It is the custom for the Hawaiian chiefs, since the times beyond tradition, to be attended by a maiden who shall minister to them in illness. Kalaua was clad in a dull gown that fitted her figure loosely, and she passed her hands softly and swiftly over the chest and limbs of her chief, as is the native manner of massage... She murmured tender words in her native tongue as she continued in her labor of love."
—Newspaper article.

96. <u>**The Dark Hills**</u>
Dark hills at evening in the west,
Where sunset hovers like a sound
Of golden horns that sang to rest
Old bones of warriors under ground,
Far now from all the bannered ways
Where flash the legions of the sun,
You fade — as if the last of days

Were fading, and all wars were done.
—*Edward Arlington Robinson*

97. **I was there when the Dead Sea was only sick.**
—*George Burns, the late actor, commenting on his advanced age.*

98. **These sudden re-integrations of tendencies opposed to homo-sexual activity in turn set up the situation of homosexual cravings, with consequences similar to those above indicated. That the outcome in these individuals who have had earlier overt experience is somewhat less ominous than is the case in its absence is not only theoretically to be expected, but actually the case both in the paranoid developments and in those who undergo schizophrenic disorders.**
—*Harry Stack Sullivan, M.D., Personal Psychopathology, p. 214.*

99. **A nervous breakdown is a relapse into auto-eroticism.**
—*Edward J. Kempf, M.D.*

100. **It was my wife Cosima Wagner who brought me here.**
—*Friedrich Nietzsche, to his guardian at the German mental hospital or asylum.*

101. **We both experience levels of ecstasy neither of us knew existed and have entered realms of intimacy, connection and devotion beyond what you dream about in your wildest fantasies.**
—*Colorado woman, writing of connecting with her "dream man" seven years after he became disabled.*

102. **Death, death, death, death at night, death in the morning, death in the afternoon. Death. We lived with death.**
—*Pavel Stenkin, Russian prisoner of war, describing his time spent at Auschwitz.*

103. **A woman in England once told me, "All people are the same to you." But that's not true. They're different but equal. I've spread my love horizontally, to cover the human race, instead of vertically, all in one place. It's threadbare, but it covers.**
—*Quentin Crisp, homosexual writer and activist.*

104. **In the case, however, of another boy, one for example who has been seriously warped by the continued or augmented**

importance of a more or less primitive attachment to his mother, and who therefore is not susceptible to any marked heterosexual drives because of attachment to the mother — with rationalizations generally contributed by her in the shape, perhaps, of advice to keep away from "bad girls," examples of misfortune resulting from dealings with crafty females, and the like – the outcome is quite otherwise.
—*Harry Stack Sullivan, M.D., Personal Psychopathology, p. 199. [The exact same outcome also pertains to daughters. - JMM].*

105. **I want to be with you!**
I want to love you and cherish you
And make you smile.
—*SNN*

106. **Galileo is revered as one of the top scientists of all time, but did you also know that he had a terrible life? At a time when everyone "knew" that the earth was flat, he proved that it was round. The church threatened him with torture if he did not recant, and to avoid that fate, Galileo did indeed recant. Did you know that after he recanted, he was kept under house arrest by the church/state for the rest of his life?**

This is the way society's leaders always treat those who seriously threaten entrenched beliefs — that comfort zone surrounding each of us. However, the church/state was only part of Galileo's problem; he was also shunned by the people of his time. I doubt that he was invited to many dinner parties.

This was brought out in the play "Galilei Galileo" by Bertolt Brecht. Before threatening Galileo with torture, the church sent a bishop to persuade him to "see reason," and "come to his senses." The bishop was kind-hearted and told Galileo that his agitation would not only put him in danger but was also very disturbing to everyone, particularly the elderly. It would crush them by shattering their lifelong beliefs, even if Galileo's outlandish discovery were true. The bishop pleaded with Galileo to show some compassion and "leave well enough alone." Galileo responded by saying that ignorance perpetuates suffering, whereas truth liberates and ultimately relieves suffering.
—*Dr. Julian Whitaker*

107. **He has finally met a girl who wants what he wants, as far as he can tell.**
—*Verlyn Klinkenborg, commenting on Samuel Hynes's book, The Growing Seasons.*

108. **During the Renaissance, the prevailing view held that gender was something easily changeable. Women were cautioned, for example, not to exert themselves too forcefully because the heat generated by extreme activity would transform their vaginas into penises.**
—*SNN*

109. **I go into my library, and all**
history rolls before me. I breathe
the morning air of the world
while the scent of Eden's roses yet
lingered in it... I see the pyramids
building: I hear the shoutings of
the armies of Alexander... I sit as
in a theatre – the stage is time,
the play is the play of the world.
—*Alexander Smith, Dreamthorp: Books & Gardens.*

110. **It was, of course, a lie what you read about my religious convictions, a lie, which is being systematically repeated. I do not believe in a personal God and I have never denied this but have expressed it clearly. If something in me, which can be called religious, then it is the unbounded admiration for the structure of the world so far as our science can reveal it.**
—*Albert Einstein, in a letter written in 1954, The Human Side, Princeton University Press, 1979.*

111. **No matter what anybody says, it all comes down to the same thing: A man and woman, a broken heart and a broken home.**
—*John Lee Hooker (1917-2001), blues guitarist and singer.*

112. **On your journey, if you come upon a canyon in your path, jump. It is not as far as you think.**
—*Native American proverb. Thanks to V. Sagar Sethi, M.D., Ph.D..*

113. **Aged Congo Street Drummer Has All of Them Beat**
        Leopoldville, the Congo. - It was the most beautiful and

spine-tingling African drumming I had ever heard. I stopped dead in my tracks - listening intently — trying to figure out where it was coming from.

The Boulevard Albert was dark and deserted. Down the street about 500 yards I could see the lights of my hotel — the Regina. I was on my way there from the Hotel Memling where several of us correspondents had stayed up past midnight rehashing the day's events.

As best I could tell, the throbbing drumbeats seemed to be coming from my side of the street — some place between where I was standing and the hotel. I started walking again, very slowly, past the darkened, shuttered shop windows. The drumming grew louder.

Suddenly I was upon it. I had come abreast of a clothing store whose display window was dimly lit by a single bulb in the corner. It was the only unshuttered shop on the street. In its recessed doorway, sitting on a dirty straw mat and clasping a drum tightly between his spindly legs, was the night watchman.

He was an old man, dressed in rags, but his hands were swift and supple as he performed his magic on the drum. I must have stood staring at him for a minute or two, hypnotized by his strange and primitive music. Then I moved to the front of the store window, pretending to be interested in the display of shirts and ties.

For a full 20 minutes I remained there motionless and listened raptly to the old man play. He was a master of his art. In his youth he must have been one of the great tribal drummers of his day.

The rhythm was slow, then fast — muted, then crashingly and wildly insistent. He seemed to be pouring out his soul through the medium of the drum. I felt like an eavesdropper — standing there intruding upon his privacy while he beat out his innermost secrets to the dark and lonely night.

It was almost with a sense of relief that I finally heard the drumming die. The old man set the instrument carefully aside and slowly stood up. He picked up a rusty tin can next to him and shuffled out onto the sidewalk and over to the grass strip next to the street. There he squatted down, built a small fire out of some trash paper and kindling and heated the food in his can.

I turned away and began walking towards the hotel. I glanced back once and saw him hunkering over the small fire, eating his dinner.

'There,' I thought to myself with the utmost sincerity, 'is one of the world's truly great musicians.'

For, you see, the drum the old man had been using was not really a drum at all — it was nothing more than an old discarded cardboard box.
—*J. Michael Mahoney, Atlanta Constitution, October 23, 1961.*

114. **Yet with all that comes a recognition of some crucial failure of generosity in herself that is partly responsible for her never having formed a lasting romantic partnership.**
—*SNN*

115. **When I married I was only half a man and could only marry half a woman.**
—*The father of a schizophrenic patient, Schizophrenia and the Family, Lidz, Fleck & Cornelison.*

116. **A great thing done is never perfect, but that doesn't mean it fails.**
—*The Minister of Leaves*

117. **Mr. Mandela was one of nine children, and his father had four wives. The family lived in a grass hut and raised livestock. The single most harrowing tale Mr. Mandela relates is not the account of his 27-year imprisonment beginning in 1963 but of his ceremonial circumcision about 30 years earlier when he was 16.**
—*Newspaper article.*

118. **How to describe David Foster Wallace's new collection of stories? You might say it's like being a therapist and being forced to listen to one narcissistic patient after the next, prattle on — and on and on — about their neuroses and their explanations for those neuroses and the rationalizations behind the explanations for those neuroses. Or you might say it's like being locked in a room with a bunch of speed freaks babbling to themselves nonstop on a Benzedrine-fueled high as they clip their toenails or cut the split ends out of their hair.**
—*Michiko Kakutani, The New York Times book reviewer.*

119. **Wall decorations on temples and tombs attest to the development of surgery in ancient Egypt. A decoration in a**

nobleman's tomb at Sakkara, dating from 2500 BC, is the world's oldest known depiction of an operation. It portrays a young man being circumcised with a stone knife, while an attendant restrains the patient's arms. "Hold him fast! Don't let him swoon!" directs the surgeon, according to the hieroglyphics nearby.
—*Newspaper article.*

120. **In any case, the appearance within awareness of the homo-erotic interest stirs such violent self-reproach that a dissociation or a vigorous defensive process results. If the self is able to dissociate the abhorrent system, the personality continues thereafter to be in grave danger of panic with succeeding schizophrenia, unless the sexual tensions are being drained off by some collateral procedure such as frequent masturbation or more or less definitely auto-sexual intercourse with women [with men in the case of females – JMM]. Moreover, under cover of the dissociation, experience in any case continues to be integrated into the dissociated system and its partition of energy in the personality to grow.**
—*Harry Stack Sullivan, M.D., Personal Psychopathology, p. 212.*

121. **Most of all the blood, my arms are up to the elbows in blood. That is the most terrible thing that lies in my soul.**
—*Nikita Khrushchev, when asked at his retirement as leader of the Soviet Union what he most regretted. He never forgave Stalin for making him an accomplice in terrible crimes. William Taubman, commenting on Nikita Khrushchev, The New York Times.*

122. **Robinson Jeffers was no scientist, but he expressed better than any other poet the scientist's vision. Ironic, detached, contemptuous of national pride and cultural taboos, he stood in awe of nature alone.**
—*Freeman Dyson*

123. **Origin of man now proved... He who understands baboon would do more towards metaphysics than Locke.**
—*Charles Darwin in pocket notebook, 1839.*

124. **I count religion to be a childish toy, and hold there is no sin but ignorance.**
—*Christopher Marlowe*

125. **I have no special talents. I am only passionately curious.**
      —*Albert Einstein*

126. **Remnick interviewed a former high NKVD officer connected with one of the Katyn-type massacres of Polish officers, who told of how the notorious Major Blokhin shot the Poles at the rate of two to three hundred a night in a soundproof room. He was dressed in a special blood-proof uniform of oilcloth, with elbow-length gloves and a sou'wester-type hat. German pistols were used, Remnick was told, because the Russian pistols tended to jam after so many shots.**
      —*Newspaper article.*

127. **I was going back to my real girl self through my pretense layers of girl on boy.**
      —*Mary Barnes, recovering from a schizophrenic breakdown (See R. D. Laing's* The Divided Self*).*

128. **IF**
      "Brother Square –Toes" – Rewards and Fairies
      If you can keep your head when all about you
      Are losing theirs and blaming it on you,
      If you can trust yourself when all men doubt you,
      But make allowance for their doubting too;
      If you can wait and not be tired by waiting,
      Or being lied about, don't deal in lies,
      Or being hated, don't give way to hating,
      And yet don't look too good, nor talk too wise:

      If you can dream – and not make dreams your master;
      If you can think – and not make thoughts your aim;
      If you can meet with Triumph and Disaster
      And treat those two imposters just the same;
      If you can bear to hear the truth you've spoken
      Twisted by knaves to make a trap for fools,
      Or watch the things you gave your life to, broken,
      And stoop and build 'em up with wornout tools:
      If you can make one heap of all your winnings
      And risk it on one turn of pitch-and-toss,
      And lose, and start again at your beginnings
      And never breathe a word about your loss;
      If you can force your heart and nerve and sinew

To serve your turn long after they are gone,
And so hold on when there is nothing in you
Except the Will which says to them: "Hold on!"
If you can talk with crowds and keep your virtue,
Or walk with Kings — nor lose the common touch,
If neither foes nor loving friends can hurt you,
If all men count with you, but none too much;
If you can fill the unforgiving minute
With sixty seconds' worth of distance run,
Yours is the Earth and everything that's in it,
And - which is more - you'll be a Man, my son!
—*Rudyard Kipling*

129. **The man who dies ... rich dies disgraced.**
      —*Andrew Carnegie, "Wealth," from the <u>North American Review</u>.*

130. **Homer's *Margites*, a humorous epic about a fool, who, in Plato's words, "knew many things, but all badly"...**
      —*Michiko Kakutani, "Books of the Times," <u>The New York Times</u>, May 6, 2006.*

131. **World War I was not only the first of the major catastrophes disrupting this century, but perhaps the worst, especially in its long-term impact. Even in an era when we have learned to count the dead in millions, some casualty figures for the Great War are still difficult to grasp. In one attack at Ypres in Belgium the British lost a staggering 13,000 men in a mere three hours, while gaining no more than 100 yards for the sacrifice. On July 1, 1916, the first day of the Battle of The Somme, the British suffered 60,000 casualties in an assault preceded by a six-day artillery bombardment of German lines. Although the Germans had been hit by three million shells along a 12-mile stretch, enough survived to offer fierce resistance. When this battle ended, total casualties amounted to over 1.1 million men. By 1918, the Allies counted 5.4 million dead and 7 million wounded; the two Central Powers suffered 4 million deaths and 8.3 million wounded.**
      —*V. R. Berghahn*

132. **Sex is quite important to me. So much so that when I'm horny my behavior tends to be irrational unless the urge is satisfied.**
      —*An anonymous female.*

133. **Anger and hate spring from frustrated sexuality.**
　　　—JMM

134. **We are nurtured or neutered by the milk our mothers feed us...**
　　　—Marie-Christine Giordano's dance company – Nurtured or Neutered.

135. **At last gleems of light have come, and I am almost convinced that species are not (it is like confessing to murder) immutable.**
　　　—Charles Darwin, in a letter nine years after his visit to the Galapagos and fifteen years prior to his book, On the Origin of Species, 1844.

136. **The civil war now being inaugurated will be as horrible as his Satanic Majesty could desire.**
　　　—Sam Houston (1793-1863)

137. **Not a few of the dead were found with their thumbs gnawed to a pulp, as they chewed them in agony before they died.**
　　　—Winston Groom, Shrouds of Glory, speaking of the 2,000 dead in the Battle of Franklin, Tennessee, November 30, 1864.

138. **Beware when the great God lets loose a thinker on this planet. Then all things are at risk. It is as when a conflagration has broken out in a great city, and no man knows what is safe, or where it will end.**
　　　—Ralph Waldo Emerson (1803-1882)

139. **...the freedom of androgynous childhood...**
　　　—Elaine Showalter, The Female Malady.

140. **And on the pedestal these words appear:**
　　　"My name is Ozymandias, king of kings;
　　　Look on my works, ye Mighty, and despair!"
　　　Nothing beside remains. Round the decay
　　　of that colossal wreck, boundless and bare,
　　　The lone and level sands stretch far away.
　　　—Percy Bysshe Shelley, The Sonnet, "Ozymandias," 1818.

141. **In nature it is always the female who woos.**
　　　—SNN

142. **The hand that rocks the cradle rules the world.**
　　　—SNN

143. **Love means never having to say anything much at all.**
      —*A. O. Scott*

144. <u>**Hilde Coppi to her mother, 1943**</u>
      **Hilde Coppi was arrested by the Nazis in September 1942,
      together with her husband, Hans, because they belonged to a
      resistance group in Germany. In prison, she gave birth to a son,
      Hans. One month later, her husband was executed. When her
      son was eight months old, Hilde was executed. She was twenty-
      four years old. Hilde wrote this letter on her last day:**

      5 August 1943

      My Mother, my dearly beloved Mama,
          **Now the time has almost come when we must say farewell
      forever. The hardest part, the separation from my little Hans, is
      behind me. How happy he made me! I know that he will be well
      taken care of in your loyal, dear maternal hands, and for my
      sake, Mama – promise me – remain brave. I know that you feel
      as though your heart must break; but take yourself firmly in
      hand, very firmly. You will succeed, as you always have, in
      coping with the severest difficulties, won't you, Mama? The
      thought of you and of the deep sorrow that I must inflict upon
      you is the most unbearable of all – the thought that I must leave
      you alone at that time of life when you need me the most! Will
      you ever, ever be able to forgive me? As a child, you know,
      when I used to lie awake so long, I was always animated by one
      thought – to be allowed to die before you. And later, I had a
      single wish that constantly accompanied me, consciously and
      unconsciously: I did not want to die without having brought a
      child into the world. So you see, both of these great desires,
      and thereby my life, have attained fulfillment. Now I am going
      to join my big Hans. Little Hans has – so I hope – inherited the
      best in both of us. And when you press him to your heart, your
      child will always be with you, much closer than I can ever be to
      you. Little Hans – this is what I wish – will become hardy and
      strong, with an open, warm, helpful heart and his father's
      thoroughly decent character. We loved each other very, very
      much. Love guided our actions.**
          **My mother, my one and only good mother and my little Hans,
      all my love is always with you; be brave, as I am determined
      also to be.**

Always,
Your daughter Hilde
—*Between Ourselves, Letters Between Mothers and Daughters*, edited by
Karen Payne, Houghton Mifflin Co., Boston, 1983, p. 204.

145.　　**Rose Schlösinger was born in 1907. Arrested by the Nazis in
Germany on 18 September 1942, because she belonged to a
resistance group, she was executed on 5 August 1943. Her
husband, Bodo, an interpreter with the German military police,
ended his life by shooting himself in a Russian farmhouse when
he learned that his wife had been condemned to death. Rose
wrote this letter to her young daughter, Marianne, the day she
was executed.**

5 August 1943

My dear little big Marianne:
　**I do not know when you will read this letter. I leave it to
Granny or Daddy to give to you when you are old enough for it.
Now I must say farewell to you, because we shall probably
never see each other again.**
　**Nevertheless, you must grow up to be a healthy, happy and
strong human being. I hope that you will experience the most
beautiful things the world has to give, as I have, without having
to undergo its hardships, as I have had to do. First of all, you
must strive to become capable and industrious, then all other
happiness will come of itself. Do not be too prodigal of your
feelings. There are not many men who are like Daddy, as good
and as pure in their love. Learn to wait before giving all your
love – thus you will be spared the feeling of having been
cheated. But a man who loves you so much that he will share all
the suffering and all difficulties with you, and for whom you can
do the same – such a man you may love, and believe me, the
happiness you will find with him will repay you for the waiting.**
　**I wish you a great many years of happiness that I unfor-
tunately could have for only a few. And then you must have
children: when they put your first child into your arms, perhaps
you will think of me – that it was a high moment in my life too
when for the first time I held you, a little red bundle, in my
arms. And then think of our evenings of discussion in bed, about
all the important things of life – I trying to answer your
questions. And think of our beautiful three weeks at the**

seashore — of the sunrise, and when we walked barefoot along the beach from Bansin to Uckeritz, and when I pushed you before me on the rubber float, and when we read books together. We had so many beautiful things together, my child, and you must experience all of them over again, and much more besides.

And there is still another thing I want to tell you. When we must die, we are sorry for every unkind word we have said to someone who is dear to us; if we could go on living, we should remember that and control ourselves much better. Perhaps you can remember it; you would make life — and later on death too — easier for you and for others.

And be happy, as often as you can — every day is precious. It is a pity about every minute that one has spent in sadness.

My love for you shall accompany you your whole life long. I kiss you — and all who are kind to you. Farewell, my dear — thinking of you to the end with the greatest love.
Your Mother
—*Rose Schlösinger to her daughter, Marianne, 1943. Between Ourselves, Letters Between Mothers and Daughters, edited by Karen Payne, Houghton Mifflin Co., 1983.*

146. **On December 12, 1994, Raymond Carl Kinnamon, convicted of shooting a Houston lounge customer, sought to filibuster his way out of his own death. He read out lists of his friends, thanked the reporters there and said at one point: I just wish I had a Shakespearean vocabulary and maybe I could express myself better. Wherever I'm buried, I'd like it to say: "Here lies a man who loved women." I've always been that way.**

After 30 minutes, officials went ahead and executed him as he spoke. His last words were: "Warden, you didn't let me finish."
—*Newspaper article.*

147. **Belief in the supernatural, especially belief in God, is not only incompatible with good science, this kind of belief is damaging to the well being of the human race...**
—*Herbert A. Hauptman, Ph.D., co-winner of the Nobel Prize in Chemistry, 1985, in "Do God & Science Mix?" by Cornelia Dean, The New York Times.*

148. **Thomas Jefferson survives...**
—*John Adams (90) on his deathbed, his last words, not knowing that Jefferson had died five hours earlier.*

149. **Time passing as men pass who will never come again**
And leaving us, Great God, with only this...
Knowing that this earth, this time, this life,
Are stranger than a dream.
—*Thomas Wolfe, In Memoriam, Frank Trippett (1926-1998).*

150. **Is it the 4th?**
—*Thomas Jefferson (83), his last words on his deathbed, on the fiftieth anniversary of the Declaration of Independence.*

151. **I believe in Spinoza's God.**
—*Albert Einstein, when asked if he believed in God. [Spinoza posited "a universe ruled only by the cause and effect of natural laws, without purpose or design."].*

152. **This is my sixth marriage, and I ain't won one yet. So I figure I'm due.**
—*Jake LaMotta, the prizefighter, to the sportswriter, Ira Berkow.*

153. **Do you want your daughter to be taught**
A skill with which she will do well?
Send her to Maria Dominga —
She's an admirable teacher!
What is her method? I shall tell:
The lass will learn, in less than a month's time,
Learn the wise art — of wiggling her behind!
—*Pero da Ponte, Galatian lyrics, thirteenth century.*

154. **Men are just dogs! We shouldn't call ourselves human, we're just dogs, dogs, dogs! They call me a dog 'cause that's what I am, but so is everybody else — hopping around from woman to woman, just like a dog.**
—*Elliot Lieblow, "Sea Cat" from Tally's Corner: A Study of Negro Street Corner Men.*

155. **At sunset in the Kalahari it is still possible to catch a glimpse of how all men once lived. Some 30 Bushmen sit in the midst of a desert, inside a circle of low grass huts, gathered around their**

hearth fires. A child cries, and a woman is there to pick it up and console it. Individuals several hearths apart converse, and their soft voices carry easily around the circle. When they laugh, the sound spreads like a ripple from fireside to fireside. They are huddled together, bodies actually touching much of the time, in what one observer has called "the human press."
—*Newspaper article.*

156. **Snails were capable of affection up to a certain point.**
—*Charles Darwin*

157. **God told the Israelites to kill all [the Midianites], men, women and children, to destroy them, and that seems a terrible thing to do. Is it? Well, that would be 10,000 people who probably would have gone to hell. But if they stayed and reproduced... then there would be one million people who would have to spend eternity in hell... So God in love, and that was a loving thing, took away a small number so that he might not have to take away a large number.**
—*On genocide as an act of charity, SNN.*

✻

158. **So, then, since knowledge might destroy us, we will have none of it. For knowledge, Phaedrus, does not make him who possesses it dignified or austere. Knowledge is all knowing, understanding, forgiving; it takes up no position, sets no store by form. It has compassion with the abyss — it is the abyss. So we reject it, firmly, and henceforward our concern shall be with beauty only.**
—*Thomas Mann, <u>Death in Venice</u>.*

159. **I am tired of fighting. Our chiefs are killed... The old men are all dead. He who led the young men is dead... It is cold, and we have no blankets. The little children are freezing to death... I want to have time to look for my children, and see how many of them I can find. Maybe I shall find them among the dead. Hear me, my chiefs! I am tired. My heart is sick and sad. From where the sun now stands I will fight no more forever.**
—*Chief Joseph, 1887 speech as he surrendered to U.S. Army officers.*

160. **Mais dans des cas pareils,**
C'est toujours la chose génitale,
Toujours! Toujours! Toujours!
—Jean-Martin Charcot, (1825-1893), [Professor Charcot is here stating that the symptoms of hysteria exhibited by his mental patients always (toujours!) stem from unconscious sexual (génitale) conflicts – JMM].

161. **Every man has reminiscences, which he would not tell to every-one but only to his friends. He has other matters in his mind, which he would not reveal even to his friends, but only to himself, and that in secret. But there are other things, which a man is afraid to tell even to himself, and every decent man has a number of such things stored away in his mind.**
—Fyodor Dostoyevsky

162. **Under social and economic pressures, it may be that some of this type marry. The sexual handicaps in their marital rela-tionship, however, are never overcome. They endure the sex act as part of their wifely "duty," regarding their frigidity as part of their "purity." Sometimes the affection is turned toward another woman, this taking the form of a rather etherealized friendship. Or again, the homoerotic interest may be on a mother-child basis, which denies the existence of any conscious sexual impulses.**
—Clara Thompson, M.D., in Personal Psychopathology, Harry Stack Sullivan, M.D..

163. **Secondly, nothing preventing, cultural and innate factors combine in the growth of the sexual tendencies to such effect that sexual excitement and felt lust come to be greatest only when the situation can be integrated collaboratively (inti-mately) with a member of the opposite sex, in such a way that the genitals of each are stimulated in the behavior toward satisfaction. This is complete heterosexuality.**
—Harry Stack Sullivan, M.D., Personal Psychopathology, p. 236.

164. **When I examine myself and my methods of thought, I come to the conclusion that the gift of fantasy has meant more to me than any talent for abstract positive thinking.**
—Albert Einstein

165.   Love alters not with his brief hours and weeks,
       But bears it out even to the edge of doom.
       If this be error, and upon me prov'd,
       I never writ, nor no man ever lov'd.
       —*Shakespeare, "Sonnet 116".*

166.   **It is instructive that [Daniel Paul] Schreber was diagnosed in his
       first illness as suffering from severe hypochondriasis; his second
       illness commenced as an "anxiety neurosis" with attacks of
       panic, then hypochondriacal delusions and suicidal depression;
       later catatonic excitement alternating with stupor. From then on
       he might well have been diagnosed variously as suffering from
       catatonic schizophrenia, paranoid schizophrenia, dementia
       paranoides, dementia praecox, monomania, chronic mania,
       involutional melancholia, paranoia paraphrenia, obsessional
       neurosis, anxiety hysteria, tension state, transvestism, psy-
       chopathy, etc.**
       —*Drs. Macalpine and Hunter in Schreber's* Memoirs of My Nervous
       Illness.

❊

167.   **The Gray Old Men**
       **January 1 [1995] marks a thousand days of Siege in Sarajevo
       where seven-year-old**
       Nermin Divovic was hit in the face
       By a Serbian sniper's bullet.
       He could be a little boy
       Sleeping in the asphalt road
       As if tired from Christmas shopping
       On a cold winter's day.
       The large pool of deep red blood
       Flowing from his face causes us
       To yell in the night for Nermin to awake
       **His blue and purple jacket, bright green pants and dirty-white
       sneakers.**
       Do you think that the old gray men who
       **Speak for peace see Nermin Divovic in themselves? Their faces
       grown pale from a thousand days of talk, their supine souls
       devoid of life?**
       The Gestapo got Anne Frank,
       The Bomb Sadako Sasaki.

The Sniper's bullet got Nermin Divovic,
Cowardice the gray old men.
—*Gerard Brooker, high school principal.*

168. **It is not the critic who counts, not the one who points out how the strong man stumbled or how the doer of deeds might have done them better. The credit belongs to the one who is actually in the arena.**
—*Theodore Roosevelt*

169. **Dear Abby: We are both 77 years old, and we have been married 53 years. First we liked each other, then we loved each other, and now we adore each other. Our problem? We would like to die together! - Hartwig & Helen in Berkeley**
—*Marin Independent Journal*

170. **Passion is always the sister of joy.**
—*French girl in* The Studies in the Psychology of Sex, *Havelock Ellis, Vol. 2.*

171. **When I get a little money, I buy books; and if any is left, I buy food and clothes.**
—*Erasmus*

172. **For the month of March brings more than plum blossoms and daffodils. According to the timeworn English adage, it's also the month of "madder-than-a-March hare" notoriety.**
—*Glen Martin, staff writer,* San Francisco Chronicle, *speaking of "love-crazed jack-rabbits" in the spring.*

173. **Sexual asceticism was the greatest good and both organized and informal opportunities for its achievement were provided. Once one had turned from the lure of the flesh, one could live quietly in a considerable measure of sanctified intimacy with a group of kindred souls. Or one could take to a dignified paranoid state and go about a slow "psychical castration." If schizophrenic phenomena appeared, this did not necessarily disable one: quite a few opportunities for utilizing this eccentricity were provided in the business of evangelism. Moreover, one might, if needs be, found an eccentric religion and often secure the necessary disciples.**
—*Harry Stack Sullivan, M.D.,* Personal Psychopathology, *p. 225.*

174. **Here's to the crazy ones.**
The misfits. The rebels.
The troublemakers. The round
Pegs in the square holes — the
Ones who see things differently.
They're not fond of rules and
They have no respect for
The status quo. You can praise
Them, disagree with them,
Quote them, disbelieve them,
Glorify or vilify them.
About the only thing that you
Can't do is ignore them.
Because they change things.
—*Apple Computer ad, 1997.*

175. **Stupid with lust.**
—*SNN*

176. **My work is complete; a work which neither Jove's anger, nor fire**
nor sword shall destroy, nor yet the gnawing tooth of time.
—*Ovid*

✳

177. **...intense and almost passionate honesty by which all his**
thoughts were irradiated.
—*Thomas Henry Huxley, in a eulogy for Charles Darwin.*

178. **I want to talk to the black men in here that's coming up in the**
hood, coming up in the struggle. We're killing each other, dawg.
And it's about nothing. Nothing. Nothing. We're all dying. And
we're leaving our kids. Our mamas. Our grandmas. Over
nothing.
—*Obie Trice, Detroit rapper during three-hour memorial service,*
Fellowship Chapel, Detroit [Note: no fathers mentioned – JMM].

179. **Hey, don't knock masturbation. It's sex with somebody I love.**
—*Woody Allen, film producer.*

180. **Not to be a Jew, he (Disraeli) proclaimed, was the real**
misfortune: "Half Christendom worships a Jewess, and the other

half a Jew... Which do you think should be the superior race, the worshipped or the worshipper?"
—*John Sutherland commenting on the book, "Young Disraeli," The New York Times Book Review, April 30, 1995.*

181. **Any moron can make money.**
       —*Alexander H. Cohen*

182. **From my material, in which negative instances are conspicuously absent, I am forced to the conclusion that schizophrenic illnesses in the male [female] are intimately related as a sequel to unfortunate prolongation of the attachment of the son [daughter] and the mother. That schizophrenic disorders are but one of the possible outcomes of persisting immature attitudes subtending the mother and son [daughter] relationship must be evident. The failure of growth of heterosexual interests, with persistence of autoerotic or homosexual interests in adolescence, is the general formula. The factors that determine a schizophrenic outcome may be clarified by a discussion on the one hand of the situations to which I shall refer as homosexual cravings and acute masturbation conflict - often immediate precursors of grave psychosis - and of the various homo-erotic and autoerotic procedures, on the other.**
       —*Harry Stack Sullivan, M.D., Personal Psychopathology, p. 211 [Italics added by JMM].*

183. **Mourning elephant dies on Valentine's Day**
       Lyon, France – Love claimed a victim at the Lyon zoo. Distraught at the death of her mate a month earlier, Pankov, the Asian elephant, rejected food for more than four weeks, finally following him in death – on Valentine's Day. Pankov's partner of 34 years, Mako, died by their cage at Tete d'Or zoo.
       —*Independent Journal News Services*

184. **May the most you wish for be the least you get.**
       —*Old Irish blessing on St. Patrick's Day.*

185. **A woman reported that her husband had called her every day at 6 a.m. for the past 30 years to wake her up. But that morning he had not called her. The husband works at a grocery store in Bon Air Center and police contacted him. The husband said he**

had gotten too busy and forgot to call. He said he will call his wife.
—*Newspaper article.*

186. **Not knowing how to listen, neither can they speak.**
—*Heraclitus*

187. **A madness most discreet, a choking gall, and a preserved sweet.**
—*William Shakespeare describing sex in* <u>Love Scents</u> *by Michelle Kodis with Deborah Houy and David T. Moran, Ph.D., 1998.*

188. <u>**Should we ban the Bible?**</u>
    Can you imagine my shock and dismay when I learned that several forms of blatant pornography are readily available to our children, at home, at school, in the libraries, and on the Internet? It is perhaps the most commonly available and over-looked source of pornography in the world, often escaping the eyes of even the most diligent of parents and teachers.
    Described in this pornography are blatantly despicable acts of rape, incest, masturbation, coprophilia, murder, infanticide and nudity, to name a few. The list of references is so long I could not begin to list them here.
    It is a crime to provide persons under the age of 18 with any form of pornography, and yet many parents are unwittingly providing their own children with this horrible stuff.
    It's time to crack down on this dreadful and disgusting source of trash. Under the law, no source of pornography is acceptable reading for a child, and it must be kept from the children's sight and grasp.
    You may have guessed by now that I'm referring to the Old and New Testaments. If you don't believe me, then check out some of the passages for yourself.
—*C. D. Nash, Sausalito, CA.*

189. **Contrary to a prevalent belief, the mother who offers little supervision of her adolescent daughter is the one who does the minimum of harm. Not only is this the case when it results from a satisfactory solution of her own difficulties, but also it is the case with all situations of apparent indifference. When permitted to exercise her own judgment, the girl has but to learn the ways of the social group in which she moves, and is freed of**

the necessity of making her life compatible with the added complications resulting from too close supervision.
—*Clara Thompson, M.D., in* Personal Psychopathology, *Harry Stack Sullivan, M.D., p. 248.*

190. **Dear Ann Landers:**
For the past few months, I have been thinking seriously about killing myself. I have tried to think of reasons not to, and the only one I can come up with is that it would cause my family a lot of grief. I am 15 and feel so alone. I am scared. I feel worthless. The problem is I am absolutely certain that I am gay. At 15, a guy should be thinking about what he wants to do in life, not how to kill himself. I have always wanted to get married and have children, but I now know that lifelong dream is impossible. If there were some pill I could take to make all these sexual desires go away, I would gladly take it. This isn't the easiest letter to write, Ann. I have nobody to talk to, and I need your advice more than anything. I can't talk to my mother because I am scared to death of how she would take it. Please, Ann, help me. I can't go on this way much longer.
—Marin Independent Journal, *date not noted.*

191. **The ordinary man cannot imagine this Providence otherwise than in the person of a greatly exalted father. Only such a one could understand man's needs, could be softened by his prayers and placated by the signs of his remorse. The whole thing is so obviously infantile, so incongruous with reality that to one whose attitude to humanity is friendly it is painful to think that the great majority of mortals will never be able to rise above this view of life.**
—*Sigmund Freud,* The Future of an Illusion *[Delusion! – JMM].*

192. **I love my breasts because they were never there before. And now, I wake up in the morning and they look at me in the mirror and say, "Hello, Leelee!" I put them away in a shirt, but I always leave a little bit showing.**
—*Leelee Sobieski, 17, actress,* Seventeen *Magazine.*

193. **More than thirty years of intensive investigation of these problems permits me to make the general statement that in man every case of emotional neurosis or psychosis is the result of more or less conflict and confusion involving bisexual dif-**

ferentiation... Dementing schizophrenia is essentially a regression to the cloacal level of hermaphrodism.
—*Edward J. Kempf, M.D., Bisexual Factors in Curable Schizophrenia, 1948.*

194. **A brilliant mind, great intellectual boldness, and an ability to combine the best qualities of a naturalist observer, philosophical theoretician, and experimentalist — the world has so far seen such a combination only once, and it was in the man Charles Darwin.**
—*Ernst Mayr (1904-2005) from One Long Argument.*

195. **How is it that we hear the loudest yelps for liberty among the drivers of Negroes?**
—*Dr. Samuel Johnson, speaking of the Americans, 1775.*

196. **Paranoia is precisely a disorder in which a sexual aetiology is by no means obvious; far from this, the strikingly prominent features in the causation of paranoia, especially among males, are social humiliation and slights. But if we go into the matter only a little more deeply, we shall be able to see that the really operative factor in these social injuries lies in the part played in them by the homosexual components of emotional life.**
—*Sigmund Freud, Notes on a Case of Paranoia.*

197. **What shows a man's age, mostly, is the lower part of his face. From the nose down to the neck. That's said to be why it's hard to judge the age of a man with a full beard.**
—*Newspaper article.*

198. **Loving relatedness means that each person is all persons and all things to the other.**
—*Harold Searles, M.D.*

199. **Now I am become Death, the destroyer of worlds.**
—*Robert Oppenheimer, paraphrasing from the Bhagavad-Gita, seconds after the first nuclear explosion in the New Mexico desert.*

200. **Twenty-four minutes of thundering hell on Iron Bottom Bay.**
—*Plaque on the USS San Francisco monument at Land's End, San Francisco.*

201. **I have never seen a man who loved virtue as much as sex.**
      —*Confucius*

202. **One thing was stunningly clear: with this achievement, the estimated number of galaxies in the Universe had multiplied enormously — to 50 billion, five times as many as previously estimated. The Sun is one of 50 billion to 100 billion stars in the Milky Way, generally considered to be an ordinary galaxy.**
      —*Newspaper article.*

203. **Field Marshal Gebhard Leberecht von Blücher served with the combined British-Prussian army that was about to whip Napoleon Bonaparte on June 18, 1815, at Waterloo. But the field marshal didn't get into that fray. Immediately after he made a short speech to his troops, he was taken into protective custody and hustled away from the front. He later retired as the most highly decorated marshal in the Prussian army. But what he said on that day in that short speech was he'd just discovered he was pregnant and about to give birth to an elephant.**
      —*Newspaper article.*

204. **And the hero who solves every riddle must have been wise not so much because of his intelligence but because his emotional freedom, unhindered by repression, enabled him to recognize the hidden truth.**
      —*American Imago, No. 3, quoted in Dr. Otto Fenichel's The Psycho-Analytic Theory of Neurosis, 1942.*

205. **Women are the driving force, and women want daughters! And they're not apologizing about it anymore. They used to call and there would be this qualification: "I love my two boys to death, but..." Now they go right to the Net. And there's no apology. It's "I live in South Jersey — where's the closest center?"**
      —*Ronald J. Ericsson, [in] "Getting the Girl" by Lisa Belkin, The New York Times Magazine, July 25, 1999.*

206. **A shuddering orgasm.**
      —*SNN*

207. **There've been many times when I'd be perspiring — I do a lot of that on stage — and I was crying. People thought I was only**

perspiring, but I'd be crying. I used to go with a girl. She also had a madam, and I used to ask her how could she do this and do that and still love me. She said, "That's my job, but with you it's love."
—*B. B. King, Musician magazine.*

208. **I'm tired of magazines**
Saying flat butts are the thing
Take the average black man and ask him that
She's gotta pack much back
Fellas (yeah) fellas (yeah)...
Tell 'em to shake it (shake it) shake it (shake it)...
—*Anthony L. Ray (Sir Mix-A-Lot) "Baby Got Back," 1992.*

209. **But now for many years I cannot endure to read a line of poetry: I have tried lately to read Shakespeare, and found it so intolerably dull that it nauseated me... My mind seems to have become a kind of machine for grinding general laws out of large collections of facts, but why this should have caused the atrophy of that part of the brain alone, on which the higher tastes depend, I cannot conceive.**
—*Charles Darwin, Autobiography.*

210. **Albert Einstein, so outwardly serene, once said that after the theory of relativity stormed into his mind as a young man, it never again left him, not even for a minute.**
—*Michael Specter*

211. **My friend, Hamilton, whom I shot.**
—*Aaron Burr, speaking of Alexander Hamilton.*

212. **Irene was constitutionally incapable of giving herself up to him body and soul.**
—*SNN*

213. **As our unheroic century limps to its conclusion, it becomes increasingly evident that he was the sort of man posterity will hold in awe for having been heroically true to himself. He gave his life for his truth...**
—*Edmund White, speaking of artist Giacometti.*

214.   **I surrendered as much to Lincoln's goodness as I did to Grant's army.**
        —*General Robert E. Lee*

215.   **Insanity is hereditary — you can get if from your children.**
        —*Sam Levenson*

216.   **I took by the throat the circumcised dog, and smote him thus.**
        —*William Shakespeare, <u>Othello</u>.*

217.   **ARBEIT MACHT FREI. (Work Will Make You Free)**
        —*Sign displayed over entrance to Auschwitz-Birkenau concentration camp in Poland. Also over gate to Sachsenhausen concentration camp near Berlin.*

218.   **In the fable, the hungry wolf envies the dog his comforts until he sees the mark of the collar and chain, which the dog explains to him:**
        "You mean you are not free to go where you choose?"
        "No," said the dog, "but what does that mean?"
        "Much," answered the wolf, as he trotted off. "Much."
        —*From <u>Aesop's Fables</u>, as recounted by Barry Holstun Lopex in his book, "Of Wolves and Men".*

219.   **"Just because I'm Albert Einstein**
        Doesn't mean I understand
        The ever-expanding universe
        Between a woman and a man
        If I knew, or had half a clue
        I'd be much more famous than I am"
        —*Albert Einstein dreams in <u>Naked to the World</u>.*

220.   **Monet, Manet. I've heard it both ways.**
        —*Discerning art lover overheard by Jeannette Herman in the Musee d'Orsay, Paris.*

221.   **From the little reading I had done, I had observed that the men who were most in life, who were molding life, who were life itself, ate little, slept little, owned little or nothing. They had no illusions about duty, or the perpetuation of their kith and kin, or the preservation of the State. They were interested in truth and in truth alone. They recognized only one kind of activity — crea-**

tion. **Nobody could command their services because they had of their own pledged themselves to give all. They gave gratuitously, because that is the only way to give. This was the way of life which appealed to me: it made sound sense. It was life — not the simulacrum which those about me worshipped.**
—*Henry Miller on writing.*

222. **Nicole Child has one for what she calls our "isn't my child sooo precious?" department. Her three-year-old Brendan saw his little girlfriend arrive at the day care center and gulped, "I think hearts will come out of me." ...and Joan Hess heard her seven-year-old niece, Elizabeth, reciting as she prepared for her first communion, "Our Father, who are in heaven, how did you know my name?"**
—*Newspaper article.*

223. **A courteous person will always make everyone around him feel at his best and most alive. No matter how superior his knowledge, his breeding and so on, he will bring to his meeting with another person an absolutely genuine interest, respect and concern for that person; and above all, he will give him his whole attention without curiosity or demand, and so immediately communicate to the other a freedom and sureness of which, perhaps, he did not know himself to be capable. The courtesy of the soul is lived only when every man as an individual person has been recognized as kin — and indeed when every animal and thing too is given the rights of kin in the oneness of creation.**
—*Helen M. Luke in* Kaleidoscope: The Way of Woman.

224. **The dead, the dead, the dead... somewhere they crawl'd to die, alone, in bushes, low gullies, or on the sides of hills — there, in secluded spots, their skeletons, bleach'd bones, tufts of hair, buttons, fragments of clothing, are occasionally found — our young men once so handsome and so joyous, taken from us.**
—*Walt Whitman, describing the horrors he had witnessed during the Civil War.*

225. **There's no secret about it, really.**
      You just don't die, and you get to be 100.
      —*Hazel Miller, 100, on getting there.*
      (Quotation of the Day, The New York Times, *October 19, 2010, p. A2).*

226. **Love looks not with the eyes, but with the mind,
And therefore is wing'd Cupid painted blind.**
—*William Shakespeare, <u>A Midsummer Night's Dream</u>.*

227. **I wanted to save him. I wanted to save him like I never wanted
to do anything in my life. But I couldn't win. I reckon I didn't
know enough. But if I had known enough, how could I have
won? How can you save someone that doesn't want to be
saved? Because he doesn't want to be saved. Not from drink,
not from loneliness, not from death.**
—*Horton Foote, <u>The Midnight Caller</u>, Philco-Goodyear Playhouse.*

228. **There is nothing fair and balanced about the truth.**
—*Lou Dobbs, CNN analyst.*

229. **It is well that war is so terrible. We should grow too fond of it.**
—*Robert E. Lee*

230. **It does seem difficult for most people to grasp that, as far as
science is concerned, our presence on earth is the result of a
series of accidents.**
—*Charles Gross*

231. **With me the horrid doubt always arises whether the convictions
of man's mind, which has been developed from the mind of the
lower animals, are of any value or at all trustworthy. Would
anyone trust in the convictions of a monkey's brain...?**
—*Charles Darwin*

232. **Sexual identity guarantees our psychic unity.**
—*Julia Kristeva, Bulgarian psychoanalyst.*

233. **Dying is personal... and it is profound. For many, the thought of
an ignoble end, steeped in decay, is abhorrent. A quiet, proud
death, bodily integrity intact, is a matter of extreme
consequence.**
—*The late Supreme Court Justice William Brennan.*

234. **If there is a worse place than hell, I am in it.**
—*President Abraham Lincoln, during the Civil War.*

235. **Speak not soothingly to me of death, O glorious Odysseus. I would choose so that I might live on earth to be the servant of a penniless man than to be lord over all the dead.**
—*"Homer," Book XI of* <u>The Odyssey</u>, *where the ghost of Achilles addresses Odysseus from the underground.*

236. **A symphony has a climax, a poem builds to a burst of meaning, but we are unfinished business. No coming together of strands. The game is called because of darkness.**
—*Allen Wheelis*

237. **The best gift a man can give his children is to love their mother. [And vice-versa for the mother! – JMM]**
—*Laura Stratham Hulka, quoting her father.*

238. **Look, Diane, Glover's here. He'll sleep with you every night, only you won't sleep at night.**
—*U.S. Army Sergeant Stephen Schap of Baltimore, upon decapitating his wife's lover, Gregory Glover, and taking the head to her hospital room.* <u>San Francisco Chronicle</u>.

239. **I AM SICK AND TIRED OF BEING SICK AND TIRED.**
—*On the tombstone of Fannie Lou Hamer, 1917-1977, a civil rights leader buried in a Ruleville, Mississippi park.*

240. **You may not be able to read this. I am writing it in a hurry. I see death coming up the hill.**
—*Written by a young American soldier just before his death on Hamburger Hill in Vietnam, 1969.*

241. **Last night the light that so brilliantly shines from our great university flickered for a moment. One of our brightest leaders and dearest friends has left us.**
—*Former chancellor Robert M. Bendahl, University of California, Berkeley, announcing the death of former chancellor Chang-Lin Tien, October 30, 2002.*

242. **Ever since then, for me, being rich is being warm.**
—*"Gloves" Greenberg*

243. **Among those who prove incapable of achieving the biologically ordained heterosexual goal are a great many to whom the mother has continued to be of excessive significance, over-shadowing or coloring strongly all prehensions of other women. This handicap is perhaps most vividly illustrated in the case of the woman who has married for spite a man whom she soon comes to loathe, yet with whom the peculiarities of her personality, or economic factors, or other cause, force her to live. When a son is born of such a union, he is generally sacrificed to the mother's unsatisfied erotic tendencies, and he becomes tied to her by the sort of intimacy so remarkably symbolized by Von Stuck in his painting, Die Sphinx. Whether he comes finally to rebel, hates her, and goes through life destroying as much as he can of that which arouses the mother stereotype, or instead goes on being her child-lover, the result is most unfortunate as to his growth in personality. It is almost certain that he will not proceed in erotic development past interest in his own sex.** *[When a daughter is "born of such a union," she is "generally sacrificed to the mother's unsatisfied erotic tendencies," thus becoming either homosexual or schizophrenic, just as with the son, depending on whether or not she tries to repress her homosexuality. – JMM]*
—Harry Stack Sullivan, M.D., *Personal Psychopathology*, p. 196.

244. **My husband [Herman] has been clinically depressed for most of his adult life. His therapist discovered that during adolescence, Herman had been a cross-dresser. He apparently had worn women's clothing in his early teens but repressed it as an adult. Herman is artistic and sensitive, a gourmet cook and an avid sportsman. [Another bearded lady example – Schreber's name is legion. - JMM]**
—SNN

245. **If God wills that it continue... until every drop of blood drawn with the lash shall be paid by another drawn with the sword, so it must be said, "the judgments of the Lord are true and righteous altogether."**
—Abraham Lincoln

246. **Where is the happy life? The natives we met in Tahiti had every natural luxury and seemed happy. The Australian aborigines with the barest of necessities were apparently happy, too. We**

Europeans with our complicated civilization are unhappy. That is the dilemma: civilization has failed because it has abandoned nature.
—*Captain James Cook, in his logbook, 1770*

247. **I don't care much for coincidences. There's something spooky about them: you sense momentarily what it must be like to live in an ordered, God-run universe, with Himself looking over your shoulder and helpfully dropping coarse hints about a cosmic plan. I prefer to feel that things are chaotic, free-wheeling, permanently as well as temporarily crazy – to feel the certainty of human ignorance, brutality and folly.**
—*Geoffrey Braithwaite, Narrator of Julian Barnes's* Flaubert's Parrot.

248. **In my youthful days, I have seen large herds of buffalo on these prairies, and elk were found in every grove, but they are here no more... For hundreds of miles, no white man lived, but now trading posts and settlers are found here and there throughout the country and in a few years, the smoke from their cabins will be seen to ascend from every grove and the prairie covered with their cornfields.**
—*Shabonee, peace chief of the Potawatomi (1827).*

❀

249. **If your mother says she loves you, check it out.**
—*Old journalism saying.*

250. **He was not graceful or elegant, nor remarkably fluent, but came out occasionally with a power of thought or expression that moved us from our seats. He was our colossus on the floor.**
—*Thomas Jefferson, describing John Adams at the Continental Congress.*

251. **Forty years ago I fought Custer all day until all were dead. I was then the enemy of the white man. Now I am the friend and brother, living under the flag of our country.**
—*Chief Two Moons, Northern Cheyenne, 1916.*

252. **Throughout there will be times of shared sadness and joy. There will be good humor and much laughter. In their most intimate moments, our happy couple will be warm and tender, sensuous and passionate, spontaneous and lustful. Most outside ob-**

servers will have no difficulty agreeing that this couple are living, or have indeed lived, a long and happy life together.
—*SNN*

253. I am of the opinion that my life belongs to the world community, and as long as I live, it is my privilege to do for it whatsoever I can. I want to be thoroughly used up when I die, for the harder I work the more I live. I rejoice in life for its own sake. Life is no brief candle to be, but a splendid torch which I have got hold of, and I want to make it burn as brightly as possible before handing it on to future generations.
—*George Bernard Shaw*

254. What his book is saying is that a boy becomes a homosexual man when the circumstances of his life deny him the other, more normal gratifications of his need for affection. [And vice-versa for the girl. – JMM]
—*Elizabeth Hardwick, commenting on the book about Truman Capote, by George Plimpton.*

255. The fury which so often boiled up in me had to do with a sexual craving (homosexuality) which would only manifest itself much later.
—*Julian Green, Autobiography, Vol. II, Marion Boyars Publishers. Translated from the French by Evan Cameron.*

256. **NO MORE TIME FOR FOOLISHNESS**
—*Bumper sticker seen on a rickety old cab, Lagos, Nigeria.*

257. Dr. Shreber, too, whose delusions culminated in a wishful phantasy of an unmistakably homosexual nature, had, by all accounts, shown no signs of homosexuality in the ordinary sense of the word.
—*Sigmund Freud, Notes on a Case of Paranoia.*

258. I do my thing, and you do your thing.
I am not in this world to live up to your expectations,
and you are not in this world to live up to mine.
You are you and I am I,
And if by chance we find each other, it's beautiful.
If not, it can't be helped.
—*Fritz Perls, In and Out of the Garbage Pail.*

259. **The scenes in this field would have cured anybody of war. Mangled bodies, dead, dying, every conceivable shape, without heads [or] legs.**
—*General William Tecumseh Sherman, in a letter to his wife about the Battle of Shiloh, 1862.*

260. **In Christ there is neither male nor female.**
—*Saint Paul*

261. **In our youths, our hearts were touched with fire.**
—*Oliver Wendell Holmes, as a Civil War veteran.*

262. **A wise person once said that "life is what happens while you are making other plans."**
—*Ronald Tauber, Ph.D.*

263. **Camus once said — I think he was writing about Nietzsche — that it is possible to spend a life of wild excitement without ever leaving your desk. The life of the mind, he meant, can be as risky and challenging as any heroic enterprise.**
—*A. Alvarez, commenting on James Salter's book, Burning the Days: Recollection.*

264. **Trapped in a car on 101**
He comes up from behind me. Circles my waist with his arms. His lips nudge against my ear. His hands begin to travel down... tracing curves... He rubs up against me. My lips swell with wetness. I feel his hardness... His breath is deeper now... "Hurry," he whispers. "I want you right here." Heat rises... in me... around me...
Car brakes slam. I jerk forward. "Damn drivers," my husband the driver mutters under his breath. Air. Hot. Thick. Surrounds us. Lines of cars. All waiting. No end in sight. My silk dress... now soaked... with desire for someone else faraway from here.
—*Nancy Sasha Long, Petaluma, The Pacific Sun.*

265. **Pope John Paul II's biggest buddy was Monsignor Stanislaw Dziwisz, who had been his friend for 56 years. Wherever the pope was, Dziwisz was usually nearby; they ate almost every meal together. "You need someone by your side, kind of soul-mate, and that is what Don Stanislaw is."**
—*Vatican aide to People magazine.*

266. **Life in Lubbock, Texas, taught me two things: one is that God loves you and you're going to burn in hell; the other is that sex is the most awful, filthy thing on Earth and you should save it for someone you love.**
—*Butch Hancock, songwriter from Lubbock.*

267. **Do what is in your heart, and you carry in yourself a revolution.**
—*Jacob, the character in Clifford Odet's play "Awake and Sing!".*

268. **Life is short. Ride your best horse first!**
—*SNN*

269. **Greetings from Nastasia to my lord, to my brother. My Boris is not alive anymore.**
—*Letter from widow of man cited above.*

270. **When this letter arrives, send me a man on a horse, for I have many things to do here. And send me a shirt. I forgot my shirt.**
—*Letter from husband to wife, written on birch bark document, mid-eleventh to fifteenth-century, near Novgorod, Russia.*

271. **[My penis feels] like an acorn with squirrelly tooth marks.**
—*James McManus, describing how he felt after a devastating divorce, before being made whole again.*

272. **The melancholy are always aggressive. They cannot speak but they must bite. But they are unaware of their own aggression and feel attacked instead. As they that drink wine think all runs around when it is in their own brain.**
—*Robert Burton, The Anatomy of Melancholy.*

273. **From Mikita to Ulianica. Marry me. I want you and you want me. Send Ignat as witness.**
—*Man to girlfriend, same as above.*

274. **True monogamy is rare. So rare that it is one of the most deviant behaviors in biology.**
—*Olivia Judson, an evolutionary biologist.*

275. **Nature, pitchfork it out how you may, keeps tumbling back in on you, slyly overbears your shying from it.**
—*Horace*

276. **A tiger's roar can be heard for several miles. It roars when a kill is made or during mating.**
—*Newspaper article.*

277. **Madly in love. Crazy about you.**
—*JMM*

278. **I detest the masculine point of view. I am bored by his heroism, virtue and honour. I think the best these men can do is not to talk about themselves anymore.**
—*Virginia Woolf*

279. **They strove to carve some meaning beyond the self from the painful raw materials of their suffering.**
—*Michael Vincent Miller, "Tom Lutz's American Nervousness, An Anecdotal History," 1903, <u>The New York Times Book Review</u>.*

280. **We know that the first step towards attaining intellectual mastery of our environment is to discover generalizations, rules and laws, which bring order into chaos.**
—*Sigmund Freud, <u>Analysis Terminable and Interminable</u>.*

281. **One must keep in mind that the distinction between a patient merely "mentally ill" and an "insane patient" is an extremely difficult one and that these forms of illness shade into one another in almost imperceptible transitions.**
—*Drs. Macalpine and Hunter, Daniel Paul Schreber, <u>Memoirs of My Nervous Illness</u>.*

282. **At night, with the birds teeming at their nests, the place is transformed by a hundred scenes of carnal bliss.**
—*George Divoky, Cooper Island.*

283. **Carnal bliss ... orgasmic rapture.**
—*JMM*

284. **Pain makes it difficult to see. It can blind you or narrow you, whether it's pain of loneliness, or physical pain or the pain of loss.**
—*Bob Kerry, Medal of Honor recipient.*

285. **Christ was either liar, lunatic, or Lord.**
—*Thomas Aquinas*

286. **Never give in, never, never, never, never – in nothing, great or small, large or petty – never give in except to convictions of honor and good sense.**
—*Sir Winston Churchill*

287. **It's a really joyous day, a big day for the people of Sierra Leone, especially those of us without feet or arms.**
—*Mohammed Bah, on the presidential elections after years of brutal war.*

288. **Seize the day – put no trust in the morrow!**
—*Horace*

289. **...a filthy little atheist...**
—*Theodore Roosevelt (1858-1919), commenting on Thomas Paine's book, "The Age of Reason," a frontal assault on Christianity.*

290. **Well, we've knocked the bastard off.**
—*Sir Edmund Hillary, commenting on having reached the summit of Mt. Everest in 1953 with Sherpa guide Tenzing Norgay.*

※

291. **<u>Grandfather Great Spirit</u>**
All over the world the faces of living ones
are alike.
With tenderness they have come up out
of the ground.
Look upon your children that they may
face the winds and walk the good road to
the Day of Quiet.

<u>Grandfather Great Spirit</u>
Fill us with the Light.
Give us the strength to understand,
and the eyes to see.
Teach us to walk the soft Earth as relatives
to all that live.
—*Sioux Prayer*

292. **Electric shock treatments "walk the thoughts right out of your mind."**
—*Maurice Nouvelle, <u>The Dinosaur Man</u>.*

293. **The Malaysian minister of culture, arts and tourism suggested last year that mass circumcision ceremonies be promoted as tourist attractions.**
—*Newspaper article*

294. **A survey taken by Carvel about what people wish for when they blow out the birthday candles found that 61 percent of all boys younger than 10 years who want to be superheroes want to be Cat Woman.**
—*Newspaper article*

295. **Goddamn you all, I told you so!**
—*H. G. Wells, request for his epitaph.*

296. **They came in darkness and they came in chains. Today we strike away the last major shackle of those fierce and ancient bonds.**
—*President Lyndon Johnson, on signing the Voting Rights Act of 1965.*

297. **They are real smart at being horses.**
—*A jockey's response when asked if horses are smart.*

❋

298. **There I saw a rebel sitting on a rock with a woman's picture in his hand as though he were looking at it, but he was dead.**
—*Pvt. Charles A. Berry, Company E, First Minnesota Volunteers.*

299. **So this time I do not appeal to rage, to pride. I do not even appeal to passion. I appeal to Reason. And together with Mastro Cecco, once more condemned to death by irrationality, suicidal insanity, I say: we need to rediscover the Force of Reason.**
—*Oriana Fallaci, journalist.*

300. **To the Editor:**
An interesting test of the "religious gene" would be to examine its effects in our close cousins the chimpanzees.
—*J.D. Hill, Huntington, NY, February 13, 2005, <u>The New York Times</u>.*

301. **[I feel] envy, nothing but furious envy at my sister, or rather of my brother-in-law, because I will never have a child.**
      —*Franz Kafka, in his diary [Freudian slip? - JMM].*

302. **A piece of burnt meat/wearing my clothes.**
      —*Jane Kenyon, author, describing her depression.*

303. **I had to pay heavily for this bit of good luck. People did not want to believe my facts and thought my theories unsavory. Resistance was unrelenting.**
      —*Sigmund Freud*

304. **<u>Arches</u>**
      Of buildings, this building,
      Frame a stream of windows
      Framed in white brick. This
      Building is fire proof; or else
      It isn't: the furnishings first
      To go: no, the patients. Patients
      On Sundays walk in a small garden.
      Today some go out on a group
      Pass. To stroll the streets and shop.
      So what else is new? The sky
      Slowly/swiftly went blue to gray.
      A gray in which some smoke stands.
      —*Payne Whitney Sanitarium*

305. **<u>Trip</u>**
      Wigging in, wigging out;
      when I stop to think
      the wires in my head
      cross: kaboom. How
      many trips
      by ambulance (two,
      count them two),
      claustrated, pill addiction,
      in and out of mental
      hospitals,
      the suicidalness (once
      I almost made it)
      but – go on?
      Tell you all of it?

**I can't. When I think
of that, that at
only fifty-one I,
Jim the Jerk, am
still alive and breathing
deeply, that I think
is a miracle.**
—*Payne Whitney Sanitarium*

306. **February 13th, 1975**
**Tomorrow is St. Valentine's:
tomorrow I'll think about
that. Always nervous, even
after a good sleep I'd like
to climb back into. The sun
shines on yesterday's new
fallen snow and yestereven
it turned the world to pink
and rose and steel blue
buildings. Helene is restless:
leaving soon. And what then
will I do with myself? Someone is watching morning
TV. I'm not reduced to that
yet. I wish one could press
snowflakes in a book like flowers.**
—*Payne Whitney Sanitarium*

307. **All truth passes through three stages. First, it is ridiculed. Second, it is violently opposed. Third, it is accepted as being self-evident.**
—*Arthur Schopenhauer*

308. **Genius lies in recognizing the obvious.**
—*SNN*

309. **Never grow a wishbone, daughter, where your backbone ought to be.**
—*Spoken by her mother to Clementine Paddleford, Food Editor, New York Herald Tribune, 1950s-1960s.*

310. **The impossible rifle-crack in the soft April dusk... I rushed out and saw him lying sideways where the bullet had knocked him. I bent over and patted him on the cheek, and said, "Martin, Martin, this is Ralph. Don't worry, it's gonna be all right." He tried to say something, his lips tried to move, but all he could do was look at me. It was like he was talking through his eyes — and what they were saying was, "It has come. It has happened."**
—*Ralph Abernathy, on the assassination of Martin Luther King, Jr..*

311. **A man goes to a psychiatrist and says he's depressed. Life is endless pain and he can't get thoughts of suicide out of his head. The therapist says, "There's a clown in town, Grimaldi. Everybody says his show is wonderful. Why don't you go see Grimaldi?" The man replies, "I AM Grimaldi."**
—*SNN*

312. **Every gun that is made, every warship launched, every rocket fired signifies in the final sense a theft from those who hunger and are not fed, those who are cold and not clothed.**
—*President Dwight D. Eisenhower*

313. **You'll find a woman who looks very old, but the noodle is still working.**
—*Gertrude Kurth, M.D., age 92.*

314. **Hurling down to the house of death so many sturdy souls.**
—*Homer, The Iliad.*

315. **Long after I'm dead — which is any day now - this film, "The Brown Bunny" will still exist... I feel much better now that I've placed this piece of work in the world.**
—*Vincent Gallo, The New York Times, August 15, 2004.*

316. **Dark, dark depression — which is black rage, of course.**
—*John B. Koffend, author.*

317. **God save the United States and this honorable court.**
—*Words recited as each court session of the United States Supreme Court opens [Separation of church and state? –JMM].*

318. **I am 28 years old and in prison for one count of statutory rape resulting from a consensual relationship with my teenage**

girlfriend. My sentence? Twenty-two years.
—*Joshua Stancil, Marion Correctional Institute, Marion, NC.*

319. **Charles Darwin was an "unbeliever in everything beyond his own reason."**
—*SNN*

320. **My husband and I had good luck almost every day of our lives, even the bad ones. Because we were together.**
—*Eden Ferniz*

321. **There's nothing more depressing than losing the fiery lust of your youth.**
—*Ad for vitamin supplement.*

322. **The man who is too old to learn was probably always too old to learn.**
—*Caryl P. Haskins, M.D.*

323. **We will all miss Dan here in the Valley, kind and generous people like him always leave a large empty spot when they move on.**
—*John Graham, Chief, Stanley Fire, commenting on the death of Dan Mahoney, Jr..*

324. **I never met a man so ignorant I couldn't learn something from him.**
—*Galilei Galileo*

325. **Give a man a fish, you feed him for a day.**
Teach him how to fish, you feed him for a lifetime.
—*Ancient Chinese proverb.*

326. **Glory is like the bed of Louis XIV in Versailles. It is magnificent and there are bugs in it.**
—*Victor Hugo*

327. **To what great a distance may 10,000 acres of electrified cloud strike and give its fire, and how loud must be that crack!**
—*Benjamin Franklin, Experiments & Observations in Electricity, Philadelphia, 1769.*

328. **They made us many promises, more than I can remember, but they never kept but one; they promised to take our land, and they took it.**
—*Red Cloud, a chief of the Oglala Sioux.*

329. **Those whom God wishes to destroy he first deprives of their senses.**
—*Euripides, 484-406 B.C.*

330. **In confidence I can assure you — with the world, it would obtain little credit — that my movements to the chair of Government will be accompanied by feelings not unlike those of a culprit who is going to the place of his execution.**
—*George Washington*

331. **In order to be addicted to bliss, you have to be sober.**
—*One anonymous female to another.*

332. **One who marries for love has good nights and bad days.**
—*Old proverb*

333. **Everything in nature is the result of fixed laws.**
—*Charles Darwin, Autobiography.*

334. **He has a dignity which forbids familiarity, mixed with an easy affability, which creates love and reverence.**
—*Abigail Adams, wife of John Adams, about George Washington.*

335. **Nothing of importance happened today.**
—*From the diary of King George III, July 4, 1776.*

336. **Much of the history we teach was made by the people we taught.**
—*A West Point adage.*

337. **I felt like anything rather than rejoicing at the downfall of a foe who had fought so long and valiantly, and has suffered so much for a cause, though that cause was, I believe, one of the worst for which a people ever fought, and one for which there was the least excuse.**
—*Ulysses S. Grant, in his Memoirs, commenting on the surrender of the Confederacy at Appomattox.*

338. **A marriage changes passion... Suddenly you are in bed with a relative.**
—*SNN*

339. **John J. Williams, 34th Indiana, last soldier killed in the Civil War.**
—*Anonymous*

340. **The great arrogance of the present is to forget the intelligence of the past.**
—*Ken Burns, filmmaker.*

341. **The element of megalomania, "the aggrandizement of the ego" as compensation for homosexual wishes...**
—*In the book, Memoirs of My Nervous Illness, by Daniel Paul Schreber.*

342. **It's not normal to be gay, and I think it's weird to think that it is.**
—*Quentin Crisp, homosexual writer and activist.*

343. **Melville's deep longing for emotional intimacy with other men.**
—*SNN*

344. **Imagination is more important than knowledge.**
—*Albert Einstein*

❋

345. **A certain portion of mankind do not believe at all in the existence of the gods.**
—*Plato, circa 400 B.C.*

346. **Share your fears with yourself and your courage with others. You will inspire people to do things that are incredible.**
—*The late Franklin D. Miller, Medal of Honor recipient.*

347. **I'll always regret that Rwandan thing.**
—*William Jefferson Clinton*

348. **What illuminates Kate is a fierce intelligence.**
—*Nicolas Martin, director, speaking of actress Kate Burton.*

349. **Glancing up at the stars and full moon, I felt anew that ancient sense of wonder at the improbability of life.**
      —*Tom Horgan, "A Holiday Made for Believing," <u>The New York Times</u>.*

350. **It is the responsibility of every human being to aspire to do something worthwhile, to make the world a better place than the one we found. Life is a gift, and if we agree to accept it, we must contribute in return.**
      —*Albert Einstein*

351. **Trying to sneak a fast ball by Ted Williams was like trying to sneak a sunbeam by a rooster in the morning.**
      —*Pitching great Bob Feller, speaking of hitting great Ted Williams in a videotaped interview, Obituaries, <u>The New York Times</u>, Dec. 17, 2010, p. B12, by Richard Goldstein.*

352. **I am sure it is from those days that I take the belief that the best of life is life lived quietly, where nothing happens but our calm journey through the day, where change is imperceptible and the precious life is everything.**
      —*John McGahern, <u>All Will Be Well: A Memoir</u>.*

✺

353. **In Claude Lanzmann's monumental nine-and-a-half hour documentary on the Holocaust, "*Shoah,*" one of the surviving leaders of the Warsaw ghetto uprising says bitterly, "If you could lick my heart, it would poison you."**
      —*Lenore Dickstein*

354. **I feel I can't have led the life I have inside, in my mind and emotions, without having it reflected in the meat. The ride I've taken has been down the third rail, the current has been boiling my vitals ever since I've been about 13, and something's got to give.**
      —*Seymour Krim*

355. **There's no time for beating around the bush.**
      —*Larisa Klemensko Riggs, May 30, 1992, cystic fibrosis patient, now deceased.*

356. **More than 99 percent of the species that have ever lived are now extinct.**
      —*Richard Leakey and Roger Lewin, <u>The Sixth Extinction: Patterns of Life and the Future of Humankind</u>.*

357. **Obstacles are those frightful things you see when you take your eyes off your goal.**
      —*Contributed by Alysha Carnell.*

358. **War is hell.**
      War is cruelty.
      There is no use to reform it.
      The crueler it is, the sooner it will be over.
      —*William Tecumseh Sherman*

359. **But I say unto you that whosoever looks on a woman to lust after her hath committed adultery with her already in his heart.**
      —*Jesus, the Sermon on the Mount.*

360. **In the middle of the journey of our life I came to myself in a dark wood where the straight way was lost...**
      —*Opening lines of Dante's <u>Divine Comedy</u> [clinical depression – JMM].*

361. **The quick-before-they-croak awards.**
      —*Billy Wilder*

362. **Whatsoever thy hand findeth to do, do it with thy might; for there is no work, nor device, nor knowledge, nor wisdom, in the grave, whither thou goest.**
      —*Ecclesiastes*

363. **You must be the change you wish to see in the world.**
      —*Mahatma Gandhi, 1869-1948.*

364. **People sleep peaceably in their beds at night only because rough men stand ready to do violence on their behalf.**
      —*George Orwell*

365. **Within this vale**
      Of toil
      And sin

Your head grows bald
But not your chin.
—Burma Shave

366. **Experience will convince you that there is no truth more certain**
   than that all our enjoyments fall short of our expectations; and
   to none does it apply with more force, than to the gratification
   of the passions.
   —George Washington, in a letter to his granddaughter on the eve of her
   marriage.

367. **I think part of my problem is that in a former life I was Freud.**
   —In a cartoon published in 1995.

368. **In 1068, a group of Norman women demanded that William the**
   Conqueror release their husbands from military service so that
   they could return home and satisfy their wives' sexual needs.
   Four centuries later, the Catholic Church determined that the
   Virgin Mary had conceived her son through her ear and decreed
   therefore that this organ be covered in public.
   —SNN

✳

369. **In the end only the wounded physician heals and even he, in the**
   last analysis, cannot heal beyond the extent to which he has
   healed himself.
   —Epidaurus

370. **Only a paleontologist with a Frenchman's sly sense of humor**
   would recall the bawdy musical "Oh Calcutta!" to describe the
   long tail of the dinosaur Diplodocus Carnegiei. That's because
   only a Frenchman would know the slang that gave the nude
   show its name, *"Oh quel cul t'as"* – meaning, as the author of
   ***"Dinosaur Impressions"* exclaims, "Wow what a nice ass you**
   have!"
   —Philippe Tacquet, Dinosaur Impressions: Postcards from a Paleontolo-
   gist.

371. **Like all great heroes, he shows us the enormous possibility of**
   true self-determination.
   —Gerald Early in speaking of Muhammad Ali.

372. **Look, men, there is Jackson standing like a stone wall: Let us determine to die here, and we will conquer!**
—General Bernard Bee, riding into the middle of the throng, pointing his sword toward the crest of Henry Hill, as told by James I. Robertson, Jr. in <u>Stonewall Jackson: The Man, the Soldier, the Legend</u>.

373. **It may be that he prehends the hostility of the woman and finds himself utterly impotent.**
—Harry S. Sullivan, M.D., <u>Personal Psychopathology</u>, *p. 192.*

374. **I would like to meet the man who, faced with the choice of either becoming a demented human being in male habitus or a spirited woman, would not prefer the latter. Such and *only such* is the issue for me. [and vice-versa for the female/JMM]**
—Daniel Paul Schreber, <u>Memoirs of My Nervous Illness</u>, *1903, p. 149.*

375. **Like all narcissists, she suffers from a basic lack of empathy.**
—SNN

376. <u>**Love Poem**</u>
One night way back
In the sixties between anti-war
Protests and pre-med studies
I wrestled with the maudlin words
Of a sleepy college student.
Deep into untouched hours
I tossed and turned
Stilted verses of loving you
Forever and holding you
Whenever it became too cold or
Dark.
And now, decades later
With children older than we were
When we met, I am still maudlin
Still loving you and still holding
You
Whenever it becomes too cold or
Dark.
—Roger Graner

377. **A psychodynamic remission. He now has insight, the product of his psychosis and the cause of his remission.**
—*J. Michael Mahoney, Schizophrenia: The Bearded Lady Disease.*

378. **David's first wife, Michal, is "the only woman in the entire Hebrew Bible explicitly reported to love a man."**
—*Robert Alter*

379. **Lies, damned lies and statistics.**
—*SNN*

380. **We are cursed with this terrible megalomania — and paranoia that in the end is the same illness. When people think they have an extraordinary mission in life, then they also believe that everyone is pursuing them.**
—*SNN*

381. **I wasted time, and now doth time waste me:**
For now hath time made me his numbering clock: My thoughts are minutes.
—*Shakespeare, King Richard II.*

382. **The computer contributes nothing essential to the life of the mind.**
—*SNN*

383. **When all is said and done, the only thing you have is what you give away.**
—*Dear Abby*

384. **In the dark of the soul, it's always three o'clock in the morning.**
—*F. Scott Fitzgerald*

385. **A woman's love of Jesus Christ is but a projected, narcissistic love of her own maleness.**
—*J. Michael Mahoney, paraphrasing Harold F. Searles, M.D., in Collected Papers on Schizophrenia and Related Subjects.*

386. **A scold's bridle is a grotesque medieval contraption used to silence "a rude clamorous woman." It comprises a metal frame**

that cages the woman's head and a bit that pushes into her mouth and clamps her tongue.
—Patrick McGrath

387. **Women apparently do experience similar sleep arousal. But while blood flow to the penis can be monitored by attaching an expandable ring, measuring blood flow to a woman's genitals is more of a challenge. Sleep erections are typically monitored to determine if erectile dysfunction is a physical or a mental problem.**
—Answer to a question about women getting erections every 90 minutes or so during the dream stage of sleep, as men do.

388. **There is no greater enemy of correct and difficult action than a clear understanding that the act can be postponed.**
—Bob Kerry, former United States Senator, Nebraska.

389. **A great empire and little minds go ill together.**
—Sir Edmund Burke

390. **I cannot pretend to throw the least light on such abstruse problems. The mystery of the beginning of all things is insoluble to us; and I for one must be content to remain an agnostic.**
—Charles Darwin

391. **Every man has the right to be stupid on occasion but comrade Macdonald abuses it.**
—Leon Trotsky, speaking of the American leftist, Dwight Macdonald.

392. **The big secret of detective work is that you've got to get somebody else to tell you what happened.**
—Lt. John Cornicello, "Brooklyn North Homicide Squad," The New York Times, April 28, 2006.

393. **Breast cancer statistics**

    Marin County, USA – 127.8/100,000 cases
    Gambia, Africa – 3.4/100,000 cases

394. **There's no instinct so unnatural that it's not inside us all.**
—James Saynor, Story Editor for BBC-TV, in his review of The Salesman by Joseph O'Connor.

395. **She has a kind of intelligence and cleverness that serves only her own vanity.**
—Said of Marguerite Duras by Noel Godin.

396. **Human beings are in a certain sense amphibious, not exclusively connected with the land, but with the sea as well.**
—Strabo, ancient Greek geographer.

397. **An Gorta Mor, The Great Hunger**
—The Irish potato famine.

398. **Persistence has always been my strong point.**
—Professor Nora Ann Colton, Drew University.

399. **I do not even want your friendship. Everything is absolutely finished between us.**
—Maurice Chevalier, to Marlene Dietrich, in an unsigned telegram.

400. **The fox knows many things; but the hedgehog knows one great thing.**
—Archilochus

401. **After all, there is nothing normal about nature.**
—SNN

402. **Passion and roguish charm can lurk behind a mighty intellect.**
—Regarding Albert Einstein

403. **He sometimes accuses her of terrible things ("You are death"), but he sees her sin as a failure of sympathy, never as betrayal.**
—Joan Acocella, <u>Secrets of Nijinsky</u>.

404. <u>**Mabel the Sweet Honey that Poured Away**</u>
—Speedy Eric
How to Avoid Corner Love and Win Good Love from Girls

The Way to Get Money: The Best Wonderful Book for Money Mongers
—The above books were written in the 1960s by Igbo (Nigerian) writers of so-called "pulp pamphlets".

405. **Clement of Alexandria ruled that no woman could reveal to a man any portion of her body unclothed, saying nudity encouraged immorality. Pongo of Nigeria forbade wives from wearing more than a string around their loins, saying clothes encouraged immorality. Which of these sage fellows was right?**
—*SNN*

406. **Patience is bitter, but its fruit is sweet**.
—*Sticker seen on orange bus, in Lagos, Nigeria.*

407. **The general doesn't know any more about politics than a pig knows about Sunday.**
—*Harry Truman, commenting on General Dwight Eisenhower.*

408. **I never give them hell. I just tell the truth and they think it's hell.**
—*Harry Truman*

409. **Rest in peace on the wings of the wind.**
—*Epitaph at the scattering of ashes.*

❋

410. **The instructor, Lt. Gamliel Peretz, began by citing the traditional morning blessing in which, he said, all Jewish men thank God for not making them women.**
—*Deborah Sontag, reporter.*

411. **In the history of psychiatry classificatory zeal has always varied inversely with psychological understanding.**
—*Drs. Macalpine and Hunter in Daniel Paul Schreber's* Memoirs of My Nervous Illness.

412. **As Ruth said, "Entreat me not to leave thee, or to return from following after thee: for whither thou goest, I will go; and where thou lodgest, I will lodge; thy people shall be my people, and thy God my God. Where thou diest, will I die, and there will I be buried: the Lord do so to me, and more also, if aught but death part thee and me."**
—*Ruth's covenant to Naomi. Ruth 1:16-17.*

413. **The whole thing was getting so big that I thought I'd either kill myself or become an alcoholic.**
—*Chuck Williams of Williams-Sonoma, commenting on the growth of his business.*

414. **You can't pray a lie.**
—*Mark Twain, <u>Huckleberry Finn</u>.*

415. **Progress might have been all right once, but it has gone on too long.**
—*Ogden Nash*

416. **In the history of psychiatry classificatory zeal has always varied inversely with psychological understanding.**
—*Drs. Macalpine and Hunter in Daniel Paul Schreber's <u>Memoirs of My Nervous Illness</u>.*

417. **A psychological depth researcher as honestly impartial and unafraid as anyone has ever been.**
—*Sigmund Freud, <u>About Arthur Schnitzler</u> (1862-1931).*

418. **It is the duty of government to protect the poor and the weak, and to secure to every child born into this beautiful world equal chances before the state and in society.**
—*Congressman William "Pig Iron" Kelley, Pennsylvania, circa 1865.*

419. **Why do you hate me? I have never done anything to help you.**
—*Wilfred Bion, British psychoanalyst.*

420. **Creeping decrepitude has crept me all the way to the crypt.**
—*The late Joel Singer, quoted by his longtime companion, James Broughton.*

421. **After Einstein published his theory, we came to see the universe as he did. Before that, his was truly a singular vision.**
—*Marco Calavita*

422. **I do not know what fate allowed me to find a couple of nice ideas after many years of feverish labor.**
—*Albert Einstein, in a letter to a fellow physicist.*

423.   **And when the time comes to die, though I chase such thoughts away, I want time to whisper one thing: My darling, I love you.**
        —Lt. Col. Dimitri Kolesnikov – of the Russian submarine, Kursk, lost with all hands at sea.

424.   **I had ambition not only to go farther than any other one has gone before, but as far as it was possible for man to go...**
        —Captain James Cook

425.   **In a new *Newsweek* poll, 84 percent of American adults say they believe that God performs miracles, and 48 percent claim to have witnessed one.**
        —Newsweek, April 2000.

426.   **There is something obscene about a living person sitting by the fireplace and believing in God.**
        —Virginia Woolf, commenting on T.S. Eliot's conversion to Catholicism.

427.   **To see what everyone else has seen, but think what no one else has thought.**
        —Albert Szent-Georgyi

428.   **Many Jewish boys confided to their parents their wish that they were girls so that their classmates would not see that they were circumcised.**
        —SNN

429.   **There is welcome relief from anxiety at the bottom of the glass.**
        —John B. Koffend

430.   **An arch is two weaknesses, which together make a strength.**
        —Leonardo da Vinci

431.   **Beneath the rule of men entirely great, the pen is mightier than the sword.**
        —Edward Lytton

432.   **So we are rid of them at last, the brutal holy Jung and his pious parrots.**
        —Sigmund Freud, 1914.

433. **Goddamn you, stop! If you go an inch further you are a dead man.**
—A British soldier to Paul Revere during his famous ride on his horse, Brown Beauty.

434. **I think that the exhilaration of falling out of love is not sufficiently extolled. The escape from the atmosphere of a stuffy room into the fresh night air, with the sky as the limit.**
—Stella Bowen after her affair with her lover, Ford Maddox Ford, ended.

435. **Children are completely egoistic: They feel their needs intensely and strive ruthlessly to satisfy them.**
—Sigmund Freud

436. **All that is necessary for the triumph of evil is that good men do nothing.**
—Sir Edmund Burke

437. **I'm going outside and I may be some time.**
—Robert Falcon Scott, on the death of Titus Oates, as he staggered out into a blizzard, never to be seen again.

438. **The entire process began with a look. A look which led the way, a suggestive path that the lovers would walk upon later, again and again.**
—Laura Esquivel, <u>Swift as Desire</u>.

439. **Education is not filling a bucket but lighting a fire.**
—SNN

440. **The substance of things hoped for, the evidence of things not seen.**
—Hebrews 11:1, New Testament definition of faith.

441. **Just as the twig is bent, the tree's inclined.**
—Alexander Pope

442. **With the confidence only a true genius can possess...**
—Otto Nauman, speaking of the economist and eminent art historian John Michael Montias.

443. **Mr. Watson, come here, I want to see you.**
—*Alexander Graham Bell, making the world's first phone call to his assistant, Mr. Watson.*

444. **He proudly proclaimed that he had tried all his life to liberate himself from the "chains of the merely personal."**
—*William Chaloupka, on Albert Einstein.*

445. **We only walk through this world but once; any good, therefore, that we can do for our fellow man, let us do it now. Let us not defer or neglect it for we shall not pass this way again.**
—*SNN*

446. **Be happy for this moment, for this moment is your life.**
—*Alysha Carnell*

447. **To stew in his [her] own juice.**
—*Dr. Harold Searles*

448. **Be kind, for everyone you meet is fighting a great battle.**
—*Philo of Alexandria, early Jewish philosopher.*

449. **Take away love and our Earth is a tomb.**
—*Robert Browning*

450. **"What do you care what other people think?"**
—*Said to Nobel physicist Richard Feynman by his wife.*

451. **As an American streetwalker once remarked to me: "I'm literally sitting on a goldmine."**
—*William T. Vollman in <u>Poor People</u>, Echo Press.*

452. **433 - Number of genes found on the X ("female") chromosome.**

   29 - Number of genes found on the Y ("male") chromosome.

453. **There is no greater hatred in the world than the hatred of ignorance for knowledge.**
—*Galileo Galilei (1564-1642).*

454. **If I knew the world was going to end tomorrow, I would still plant this little pear tree.**
—*SNN*

455. **The truth, how can we stand it, or stand for it... one cannot help noticing that they who have a hopeless passion for truth are left largely alone – when nothing worse can be inflicted upon them.**
—*Terence O'Carolan, April 16, 1953.*

456. **I want all the cultures of all lands to be blown about my house as freely as possible. But I refuse to be blown off my feet by any.**
—*Mahatma Gandhi*

457. **You have to struggle to stay alive and be of use as long as you can.**
—*Daniel Berrigan*

458. **Frame your mind to mirth and merriment, which bars a thousand harms and lengthens life.**
—*William Shakespeare*

459. **In most hearts, there is an empty chamber, waiting for a guest.**
—*Nathaniel Hawthorne*

460. **Never argue with a fool. People might not know the difference.**
—*SNN*

461. **I felt like a bird out of a cage. Amen! Amen! Amen!**
—*Houston Holloway (1865), who had been sold three times before the age of 20, recalling his emancipation. Reported by Jay Winiki.*

462. **The sign of a great man is that the closer you get, the greater he seems.**
—*Chofetz Chaim, nineteenth - century Jewish sage.*

463. **...and during the whole of his psychosis, preoccupation with his body played a major role, as indeed it does in most psychotic patients.**
—*Drs. Macalpine and Hunter, referring to Daniel Paul Schreber.*

464. **I carry with me a level of sadness so profound that it will be with me forever.**
—*Verhoeven*

465. **It revealed America's need to blame someone rather than to accept tragedy and cope with the truth of our relative power-lessness against nature.**
—*Elinor Burkett, <u>The Gravest Show on Earth</u>.*

466. **We who have a voice should speak for the voiceless.**
—*Archbishop Oscar Romero, El Salvador, later assassinated.*

467. **She's what used to be called a sociopath and is now called antisocial personality disorder... In non-technical dialogue, she's the consummate con artist with what I'd call a hysterical personality disorder. She's like a drama queen. Everything's overdone and flamboyant.**
—*SNN*

468. **They've got us surrounded again, the poor bastards.**
—*SNN*

469. **The most extreme agony is to feel that one has been utterly forsaken.**
—*Bruno Bettelheim*

470. **Mother Nature is a drag queen.**
—*Peter Boruchowitz, 48, participant in annual gay pride parade, New York City, June 26, 2006, as reported in <u>The New York Times</u>.*

471. **The art of prophecy is difficult, especially with regard to the future.**
—*Mark Twain*

472. **Everyone is entitled to his own opinion, but not his own facts.**
—*Daniel Patrick Moynihan*

473. **Long on platitudes, short on specifics.**
—*JMM*

474. **Kindness to all living things is the true religion.**
—*Buddha*

475. **Where id was, there ego shall be.**
—*Sigmund Freud, speaking about the benefits of psychoanalysis.*

476. **In my life as a city dweller, I have crossed dark nighttime streets so as not to make the white woman walking in front of me feel fear... What I mean is that so much care, so much care is taken not to scare white people simply with my existence, and it's as if they don't want to deal with the care, too.**
—*Hilton Als*

477. **My mother is my father.**
—*A schizophrenic man.*

478. **There is so much Devil in the best of us, and so much Angel in the worst of us, that it doesn't become any of us to say much about the rest of us.**
—*W. C. Childs, copyright 1904.*

479. **Religion is the sign of the oppressed; it is the opium of the people.**
—*Karl Marx*

480. **Uncommon valor was a common virtue.**
—*Admiral Chester Nimitz, World War II.*

481. **Cavorting beasties.**
—*Anton van Leeuwenhoek, inventor of the microscope, when asked what he saw in his first slide.*

482. **...the natural world would be restored, naturally, when the last king could be strangled by the entrails of the last priest...**
—*Denis Diderot, French philosopher, 1713-1784.*

483. **Tho' the dark be cold and blind,**
Yet her sea-fog's touch is kind,
And her mightier caress
Is joy and the pain thereof;
And great is thy tenderness,
O cool, grey city of Love!
—*George Sterling, poet, writing about San Francisco, 1923.*

484. **My numerous personalities, which I refer to as "my guys" are the result of severe sexual abuse as a child. They include a six-year-old named Mozart, four-year-old twins named Anna and Trudi, and a 30-year-old seducer named Stroll.**
—Cameron West, author *First Person Plural: My Life as a Multiple*.

485. **This is ambivalence bordering on schizophrenia.**
—SNN

486. **The most incomprehensible fact about the Universe is that it is comprehensible.**
—Albert Einstein

487. **More data from such investigations may reveal that schizophrenic women, as well as men, continue in a state of non-resolution of an early type of infantile attachment to the mother, in turn re-symbolized or displaced on the father.**
—Clara Thompson, M.D., *Personal Psychopathology*.

488. **My theology is a simple muddle; I cannot look at the universe as the result of blind chance, yet I can see no evidence of beneficent design, or indeed of design of any kind, in the details.**
—Charles Darwin, on the verge of publishing *The Descent of Man*.

489. **Don't worry, dear, the sex will last only a year.**
—English mother to daughter on wedding day.

❀

490. **It's better to be mad, the mad don't see.**
—Schizophrenic patient while hiding her eyes with her hand.

491. **[Science] is such an impertinently litigious Lady that a man had as good be engaged in lawsuits as to have to do with her. I found it so formerly and now I no sooner come near her again but she gives me warning.**
—Sir Isaac Newton

492. **[It was the] happiest thought of my life...**
—Albert Einstein on first realizing that gravity was equivalent to acceleration - an idea that would underlie his new theory of gravity. As told by Alan Lightman.

493. **Characteristically, catatonic patients have the ambivalent wish to change themselves or feel that they have been transformed into another sex.**
—SNN

494. **It was St. Augustine who once and for all solidified the church's prohibition against suicide. The estates of those who killed themselves were confiscated, and a stake was driven through their bodies to keep them from rising up and haunting others with their unquiet spirits. Their bodies were buried at cross-roads under rocks.**
—Dinita Smith, The New York Times, *July 31, 1999.*

495. **But all this agrees with the fact that the sexual passion is the kernel of the will to live.**
—Arthur Schopenhauer

496. **One of our joys was to go into our workroom at night; we then perceived on all sides the feebly luminous silhouettes of the bottles or capsules containing our products. It was really a lovely sight. The glowing tubes looked like faint, fairy lights.**
—Madame Marie Curie, describing the effect of radium.

497. **These laid the world away; poured out the red**
Sweet wine of youth; gave up the years to be
Of work and joy, and that unhoped serene
That men call age; and those who would have been
Their sons, they gave, their immortality
—Lieutenant Rupert Brooke, young English poet.

498. **The weaker the ego, the more likely it is that the lust will be experienced as a function not of the self but of the introject – as something alienly lustful and further contradictory of the person's own sexual identity, such that the boy may sense a lustful female within him, or the girl, a lustful male.**
—Harold Searles, M.D., Schizophrenia & Related Subjects.

499. **Work only tires a woman, but it ruins a man.**
—Old African proverb.

500. **I know not with what weapons World War III will be fought, but World War IV will be fought with sticks and stones.**
      —*Albert Einstein*

501. **The perfect is the enemy of the good.**
      —*Voltaire*

502. **OKAY...WE'LL GO.**
      —*General Dwight D. Eisenhower, launching the D-Day invasion of Europe, June 5, 1944, 4:15 AM.*

503. **Those who have served the revolution have plowed the seas.**
      —*Simon Bolivar, about what he had come to believe was an ungovernable continent.*

504. **Sometimes I just get all hunkered up like a jackass in a hailstorm.**
      —*President Lyndon B. Johnson speaking to British Foreign Secretary, Michael Stewart, about the war in Vietnam.*

505. **Baebhen — whose name is Gaelic for "sweet, beautiful woman and melodious" — now takes a light dose of anti-rejection drugs.**
      —*SNN*

506. **Sure, I love my family, but nothing will ever take the place of my job.**
      —*Career woman to psychotherapist.*

507. **With money in your pocket, you are wise and you are handsome and you sing well, too.**
      —*Yiddish proverb.*

508. **Ninety percent of the game is half mental.**
      —*Yogi Berra, The Yogi Book.*

509. **Bury me standing. I've been on my knees all my life.**
      —*As told to Isabel Fonseca, doing her research for Bury Me Standing, her book about gypsies, in explaining the book title.*

510. **Sex is messy, passionate, unclear, tentative, anxious, liberating, frightening, embarrassing, consoling and cerebral. It's contradictory, different for different people and different for the same**

person at different times. It operates at three or four levels simultaneously. And all that covers only masturbation.
—*Pepper Schwartz, Professor of Sociology at the University of Washington.*

511. "Great God, this is an awful place and terrible enough for us to have laboured to it without the reward of priority. ...Now for the run home and a desperate struggle. I wonder if we can do it." The run home meant eight hundred miles of man-hauling [the sledges] over dreadful terrain, on increasingly short rations, in freakishly cold weather, and in the end they did not do it.
—*"S&M at the Poles," A. Alvarez, <u>The New York Review of Books</u>, 9/27/2007, p. 81 [When Robert Falcon Scott and his men arrived at the pole, they found a black flag which had been planted there earlier by the Norwegian explorer Roald Amundsen and his team].*

512. He don't smoke, he don't drink, he don't chase after women, he don't win.
—*Casey Stengal, baseball manager, commenting on an under-performing pitcher.*

513. I opted for surprise with my first pregnancy, and long after the birth I was numb that Emma was a boy. When I looked at my son, adorable though he was, I saw a stranger. The surprise was layered with guilt and stirred by hormones, in all an explosive combination. I cried on and off for weeks.
—*Kristie Andrews, "Getting the Girl" by Lisa Belkin, <u>The New York Times Magazine</u>, July 25, 1999.*

514. I do not think we can hope for any better thing now. We shall stick it out to the end, but we are growing weaker, of course, and the end cannot be far.
It seems a pity, but I do not think I can write more.
R. Scott
For God's sake look after our people.
—*The last written words of Robert Falcon Scott, Arctic explorer.*

515. You come into life with advantages which will disgrace you, if your success is mediocre. If you do not rise not only to the head

of your Profession, but of your Country, it will be owing to your own Laziness, Slovenliness, and Obstinacy.
—*John Adams to his son John Quincy Adams, in <u>The Rise of American Democracy: Jefferson to Lincoln</u>, by Sean Wilentz.*

516. **Narcissistic brittleness.**
—*JMM*

517. **The wildest colts make the best horses.**
—*Themistocles, 524-460 BC.*

518. **So, naturalists observe, a flea**
Hath smaller fleas that on him prey
And these smaller still to bite 'em
And so proceed ad infinitum.
—*Jonathan Swift*

519. **Have you shaved because you are disappointed you were created a man instead of a woman?**
—*Diogenes, his favorite question to ask a clean-cut youth.*

520. **There are no ugly women, only lazy ones.**
—*Helena Rubenstein*

521. **A book that "can be wielded like a pickax to shatter the frozen sea within the reader's mind."**
—*From a book review.*

522. **If I should die, think only this of me**
That there's some corner of a foreign field
That is forever England.
—*Rupert Brooke, <u>The Soldier</u> (He died before he saw combat.).*

523. **Great minds have always encountered violent opposition from mediocre minds.**
—*Albert Einstein*

524. **A neurosis is the negation of a perversion.**
—*Sigmund Freud*

525. **When I hear of an extraordinary man, good or bad, I natural-ly...inquire, who was his mother?**
—John Adams, 1784.

526. **...like the proverbial duck in the pond: seemingly placid on the surface but furiously paddling underwater.**
—Stuart Elliott

527. **The son of a former FBI agent was found guilty yesterday of killing two college students in a crime he confessed to his father.**

   After hearing arguments in the penalty phase, the jury then sentenced Andrew Cook, 24, to the electric chair for the January 1995 shootings of Michele Cartagena, 19, and Grant Hendrickson, 22. They were killed in a car at a lover's lane.

   Cook's father, John, testified Wednesday that it "wrenched my heart out" to hear his son admit to what was then a murder mystery. His son told him he killed the couple as they sat in Cartagena's new Honda Civic, a Christmas present from her parents the week before, Cook said.

   "He said, 'I pulled in, the car was already there and I just stopped and shot them,'" Cook said. "Then he was crying even more and he said, 'It wasn't me, Daddy. It wasn't me.... It was somebody or something that took over me'"

   After finishing his testimony, John Cook left the stand and mouthed "I'm sorry" to the victims' families seated in the front row of the courtroom.
—Newspaper article.

528.   **Whenever something goes wrong around us, it's part of our human nature to look for someone to blame — to find a scapegoat. Sometimes we point at others to keep from being blamed ourselves. (Usually, though, we just choose an easy target — someone we don't like much anyway, or someone it's easy to imagine doing wrong.)**

   Laying blame gives us the illusion of putting our world back in order. It can also relieve our own guilt, explain the unexplainable and provide an outlet for anger. But each time we lay blame mistakenly — each time we find a scapegoat — we only demean ourselves and put off addressing the real problem.
—SNN

529. **Read, read, read. Read everything.**
      —*William Faulkner*

530. **Yo' ain't the man yo' mamma wuz...**
      —*Chicago wall graffiti, 1971.*

531. **Unlike much of the rest of the world, Americans do not prefer boys. Of the first 111 Microsoft attempts, 83 were for girls.**
      —*Lisa Belkin, "Getting the Girl," <u>The New York Times Magazine</u>, July 25, 1999.*

532. **A learned fool is more foolish than an ignorant one.**
      —*Molière, <u>Les Femmes Savantes</u>.*

533. **She feared her own growing obsession. "Will I go psycho and not eat right? ...I'm afraid that if I have this baby and it is a boy I may then have postpartum depression."**
      —*Kristie Andrews, "Getting the Girl" by Lisa Belkin, <u>The New York Times Magazine</u>, July 25, 1999.*

534. **Enjoy your life as if you are to live forever, and live your life as if you are to die tomorrow.**
      —*Iman Ali, the fourth caliphate of Islam.*

535. **Dear Mr. Ferguson,**
      Thank you for your note about the possibility of a visit. Figure it out. There's only one of me and ten thousand of you. Please don't come.
      Sincerely,
      —*E.B. White*

536. **Both partners, in fact, demand a more compatible and intimate bond, rejecting the strange, impersonal, quibbling, nagging marriages so many of our parents took for granted.**
      —*Leslie Aldridhe Westoff, <u>The New York Times Magazine</u>, August 10, 1975.*

537. **There is nothing worse than an invertebrate publisher.**
      —*James M. Cox, publisher, governor, and congressman, the Democratic presidential candidate in 1920.*

538. **Dead shepherd, now I find your saw of might, Who ever loved that loved not at first sight.**
—*William Shakespeare, <u>As You Like It</u>, quoting from the poet Christopher Marlowe.*

539. **Sylvia Plath accused her mother of being "a walking vampire" who killed her father by "marrying him too old" and "burying him every day since in her heart, mind and words;" "a murderess of maleness," "a killer" as "deadly as a cobra under the shiny green gold hood."**
—*<u>The Unabridged Journals of Sylvia Plath: 1952-1960</u>, Edited by Karen V. Kukil, Anchor Books.*

540. **She acts volcanically, as any heart does when it pumps with love. She is pure emotion, naked, shameless, unmediated by discretion. These aren't attitudes of passion; this is the genuine article, take it or leave it. Even with our quibbles, we'll take it, and embrace it as tenderly as Bess does the man whose happiness she'd die for. In its pagan fervor, this is an almost religious experience.**
—*Richard Corliss, commenting on Emily Watson's performance in the movie "Breaking the Waves".*

541. **It is conceivable that maternal hostility created sex-identity problems in the children, which were solved by opting in part for the opposite sex approach to life.**
—*David C. McClelland and Norman F. Watt, "Sex-Role Alienation in Schizophrenia," <u>Journal of Abnormal Psychology</u>, 1968.*

542. **...a living mass of ruined matter...**
—*Newspaper comment on William Henry Harrison, Whig candidate for president in 1840, on being too old for the job.*

543. **He stood by me when I was crazy and I stood by him when he was drunk, and now, sir, we stand by piece each other always.**
—*William Tecumseh Sherman, commenting on his relationship with Ulysses S. Grant.*

544. **Grandmothers don't have to be smart, they only have to answer questions like "Why isn't God married?"**
—*SNN*

545. **Science is an alliance of free spirits in all cultures rebelling against the local tyranny that each culture imposes on its children.**
—*Freeman Dyson*

546. **Always go to other people's funerals, otherwise they won't go to yours.**
—*Yogi Berra*

547. **Some books are to be tasted, others to be swallowed, and some few to be chewed and digested.**
—*Francis Bacon*

548. **There will be a Jewish problem as long as the Jews remain. It is a fact that the Jews are fighting against the Catholic Church, persisting in free thinking and are the vanguard of godlessness, Bolshevism and subversion.**
—*August Cardinal Hlond, Poland, 1936.*

549. **It is better to die on your feet than live on your knees.**
—*Emiliano Zapata, Mexican revolutionary hero.*

550. **Absence is death's cousin.**
—*Dalia Sofer, in The September of Shiraz.*

551. **For instance, I read how God met Moses at an inn and sought to kill him, and how He was appeased at the last moment by the offering of a foreskin.**
—*Exodus 4:24-26.*

552. **One wife on her own is trouble. When there are several, they are forced to be polite and well behaved. If they misbehave, you threaten that you'll take another wife.**
—*Moustafa Djaara, living in France with two wives.*

553. **In these situations lies an important factor for development of serious mental disorder; and the disorder of prime importance in adolescence is schizophrenia.**
—*Clara Thompson, M.D., Personal Psychopathology.*

554a. **I am not united, I am not friendly to myself, I bite & tear myself. I am ashamed of myself. When will the day dawn of peace reconcilement when self-united & friendly I shall display one heart & energy to the world?**
—*Ralph Waldo Emerson*

554b. **Chastity - the most unnatural of all the sexual perversions.**
—*Aldous Leonard Huxley (1894-1963).*

554c. **The greatest of our evils and the worst of our crimes is poverty.**
—*George Bernard Shaw (1856-1950).*

555.

**In
Peacock
strut,
she
spread
her
wings
so
wide
that
even
to
her
mate
it
seemed
as
though
she
voiced
the
thoughts
of
evensong.**
—*Hilary Morgan, 12, 1971.*
[Note: Only males do this – JMM]

556. **Well folks,**
You'll soon see
A baked Appel.
—*George Appel, before being put to death by electric chair in 1928 for killing a New York policeman.*

557. **If you don't plan sex, you're not going to have sex.**
—*Advice to women by an author, not noted.*

558. **Being by the law of their existence as the stupidest party.**
—*John Stuart Mill, describing the Conservative Party of England.*

559. **The paranoia of blacks and whites boils up from the unrea-**
soning fear and anger of people buffeted by forces they do not
understand.
—*SNN*

560. **His face full of years.**
—*Manohla Dargis, speaking about entertainer Neil Young.*

561. **...How fatal it has been that all the women have ruled the men**
right out of their masculinity, independence, courage, will and
at last, brains even.
—*Walker Evans, photographer, reflecting on a visit to a reunion of his mother's relatives, in* Walker Evans, *by James R. Mellow.*

562. **To bear all naked truths and to envisage circumstance all calm —**
that is the top of sovereignty.
—*Said of Sigmund Freud.*

563. **If you talk to God, you are praying.**
If God talks to you, you have schizophrenia.
—*Thomas Szasz*

564. **Darwinian naturalism (the combination of metaphysical**
naturalism with Darwinian evolution) implies that the whole
point and function of our minds is to enhance reproductive
fitness; it is not to enable us to acquire true beliefs.
—*Alvin Plantigna, professor of Philosophy, Notre Dame University.*

565. **As for myself I believe that I have acted rightly in steadily**
following and devoting my life to science. I feel no remorse

from having committed any great sin, but have often and often regretted that I have not done more direct good to my fellow creatures. My sole and poor excuse is much ill health and my mental constitution, which makes it extremely difficult for me to turn from one subject or occupation to another. I can imagine with high satisfaction giving up my whole time to philanthropy, but not a portion of it; though this would have been a far better line of conduct.
—*The Autobiography of Charles Darwin.*

566. In Aeschylus's *Agamemnon,* the first play, four words — "female's male-minded eager heart" — becomes twenty-four words in poet Ted Hughes's translation from the Greek:
A man's heart in a woman's body,
A man's dreadful will in the scabbard of her body
Like a polished blade. A hidden blade.
...whose downward spiral into suicidal madness.

567. The death of youth and promise, the wasted, unlived lives — it seems too cruel to be endured.
—*Samuel Hynes, professor emeritus of literature, Princeton University, The Soldier's Tale: Bearing Witness to Modern War.*

568. I want a tough old bird with a shatterproof ego.
—*Personal ad placed by female.*

569. [The ideal American woman is] a female with a pair of buttocks in her brassiere.
—*Jean-Pierre Melville*

570. All women, as authors, are feeble and tiresome. I wish they were forbidden to write, on pain of having their faces deeply scarified with an oyster shell.
—*Nathaniel Hawthorne, in a letter to his publisher.*

571. The name syphilis comes from a poem, written by the physician Girolamo Fracastoro in 1530, about a shepherd named Syphilus who offended the god Apollo and was punished with the world's first case of the pox.
—*SNN*

572. **Was it bad for you, too?**
     A new survey has found most Americans believe other problems in life can be linked to sexual difficulties. Depression, extra-marital affairs and divorce can all be caused by poor sex, said 91 percent of the respondents to the National Institutes of Mental Health/Columbia University.
     —*SNN*

573. **Let us hope that that Mr. Darwin's theory is not correct; but if it is correct, let us hope that it does not become widely known.**
     —*Lady Ashley, well-known English aristocrat, commenting on Charles Darwin's theory of evolution.*

574. **When you sell a man a book, you don't sell him 12 ounces of paper and ink and glue – you sell him a whole new life.**
     —*Christopher Morley*

575. **20th November 1831. Went to church and heard a very stupid sermon, and afterwards took a long walk...**
     —*Charles Darwin, Journal of Researches, 1839.*

576. **Go on, get out!   Last words are for fools who haven't said enough.**
     —*Karl Marx's final words before dying.*

✳

577. **You and I ought not to die, before we have explained ourselves to each other.**
     —*John Adams, in a letter to Thomas Jefferson.*

578. **For example, a schizophrenic youth attributed his collapse to masturbation now given up but evident to him as the cause of the rather full veins upon the back of his hands.**
     —*Lewis B. Hill, M.D., Psychotherapeutic Intervention in Schizophrenia, p. 101.*

579. **I shall ask for the abolition of the punishment of death, until I have the infallibility of human judgment demonstrated to me.**
     —*Thomas Jefferson*

580. **Our sex drive does not differentiate due to reproduction instinct (so we can multiply) mixed with too much brain capabilities and not enough control over them.**
      —*Dan Bavosa, dead by suicide at age twenty-three.*

581. **God, don't let me die. I have so much to do.**
      —*Huey Long on his deathbed, just before he died.*

582. **Though the theory is worthless without the well-observed facts, the facts are useless without the frame of the theory to receive them.**
      —*Charles Darwin, autobiography.*

583. **As the daughter of a brave military man who served two tours in Vietnam, I have learned to be skeptical of wars justified by a theory espoused by men who have never seen or smelled or felt the terror of war.**
      —*Laura Whiddon Shortell, letter to* <u>*The New York Times*</u>*, February 8, 2004.*

584. **This is probably not the book for you if you want stories about cerebral oddballs who stay up all night racing for Nobel Prizes.**
      —*David Papineau*

585. **My mind is like a piece of steel, very hard to scratch anything on it and almost impossible after you get it there to rub it out.**
      —*Abraham Lincoln, in a letter to a friend. (David Bromwich, "How Lincoln Won,"* <u>*The New York Review of Books*</u>*, October 19, 2006, p. 46).*

586. **Conversation enriches the understanding, but solitude is the school of genius.**
      —*Edward Gibbon*

587. **Confusion to the British!**
      —*A toast heard at the table of George Washington during the American Revolutionary War.*

588. **Love is a communion of souls. Physical passion ignites a spark that paradoxically can release one's soul and take one beyond the physical. This is the "Law of Love."**
      —*Laura Esquivel,* <u>*The Law of Love*</u>*.*

589. **It was time for someone to stand up – or, in my case, sit down. I refused to move.**
—*Rosa Parks*

590. **When I was your age I lived with a great dream. Then the dream divided one day when I decided to marry your mother [Zelda] after all, even though I knew she was spoiled and meant no good to me.**
—*F. Scott Fitzgerald, to his daughter.*

591. **Christianity has only made one half of the world fools and the other half hypocrites.**
—*Thomas Jefferson, author of the Declaration of Independence.*

592. **Do not worry about me as everybody has to leave this earth one way or another, and this is the way I have selected. If after this terrible war is over, the world emerges a saner place ... pogroms and persecutions halted, then I'm glad I gave my efforts with thousands of others for such a cause."**
—*Sgt. Carl Goldman, a B-17 gunner killed in action in World War II, in a letter home to his parents. Sgt. Goldman was awarded a Congressional Medal of Honor, posthumously.*

593. **Calm yourself. One may be beaten by my army without dishonor.**
—*Napoleon Bonaparte, to a ranting, wounded Russian major asking to be shot because of his battlefield failure.*

594. **...a goodly number of scientists are not only narrow-minded and dull, but also just plain stupid.**
—*James Watson, co-discoverer with Francis Crick of DNA, 1953.*

595. **An auto-erotically motivated bisexuality might then be said to be universal among the young of these several species and certainly, as by Stekel, to characterize civilized man.**
—*Harry Stack Sullivan, M.D., <u>Personal Psychopathology</u>, p. 235.*

596. **I now realize my destructive suicidal despair was bound up with my denial of my body.**
—*Mary Barnes*

597. **When we have done our best, we should wait the result in peace.**
—*John Lubbock, nineteenth-century statesman.*

598. **Give me the child until he is 7, and I will show you the man.**
—*Jesuit maxim*

599. **When she was in her 90's and her daughter, my mother-in-law, delicately asked her where she wanted to be buried, Nana said, "Surprise me."**
—*Michelle Slatalla, "Online Shopper," The New York Times, September 28, 2006, p. E6.*

600. **Great geniuses have the shortest biographies. Their cousins can tell you nothing about them. They lived in their writings, and so their house and street life was trivial and commonplace.**
—*Ralph Waldo Emerson, quoted in "The Emperor's Children," reported by Joyce Carol Oates, The New York Review of Books, p. 29, October 5, 2006.*

601. **Psychotropic drugs "remove the more florid symptoms of mental illness while leaving the disturbance itself untouched."**
—*Dr. Mortimer Ostow, psychiatrist, psychoanalyst, and neuroscientist, 1918-2006.*

602. **Look, call it denial if you like, but I think what goes on in my personal life is none of my own damn business.**
—*New Yorker cartoon, patient to his therapist.*

603. **Analysis: two or three cataracts have fallen from my eyes. A hundred more to go?**
—*Susan Sontag*

604. **The greatest failing: lack of whole-heartedness.**
—*Susan Sontag*

605. **Poetry is the achievement of the synthesis of hyacinths and biscuits.**
—*Carl Sandburg, "Poetry Considered," Atlantic Monthly, March, 1923.*

606. **There's a reason you have two ears and only one mouth.**
—*George Newman, as reported by Todd A. Stottlemyer.*

607. **Hippolyte says, blessed is the mind with something to occupy it other than its own dissatisfactions.**
—*Susan Sontag*

608. **And if tormented and in anguish man is mute, God granted me to tell of what I suffer.**
—*The epigraph at the beginning of Daniel Paul Schreber's* <u>Memoirs of My Nervous Illness</u>, *translated from the German by Drs. Ida Macalpine and Richard A. Hunter.*

609. **Truth rides the arrow of time.**
—*Susan Sontag*

610. **"She had a very manly brain."**
—*Vera Atkins, as described by a colleague, in* <u>A Life in Secrets</u>, *by Sarah Helm.*

611. **"So you're the little woman who wrote the book that started this great war."**
—*Abraham Lincoln to Harriet Beecher Stowe, author of* <u>Uncle Tom's Cabin</u>, *when they met in 1862.*

612. **Writing, the art of communicating thoughts to the mind, through the eye, is the great invention of the world.**
—*Abraham Lincoln*

613. **Be regular and ordinary in your life, like a good bourgeois, so that you may be violent and original in your work.**
—*Gustave Flaubert, 1821-1880. (This quote was posted on the work-room door of the novelist William Styron, as reported in his obituary in* <u>The New York Times</u>, *November 2, 2006).*

614. **Every day, we walked into the city and dug into basements and shelters to get the corpses out as a sanitary measure. When we went into them, a typical shelter, an ordinary basement, usually, looked like a streetcar full of people who'd simultaneously had heart failure. Just people sitting there in their chairs, all dead.**
—*The author Kurt Vonnegut, describing his experiences as a prisoner-of-war in World War II, during the bombing of Dresden.*

615. **"...taking the westbound."**
—*The American "hobo" term for death.*

616. **Keep our boys clean; not only from the ravages of the liquor traffic, but the scarlot (sic) women as well... Protect them from these foes that are more deadly than the armies of Europe.**
*—A petition sent to President Woodrow Wilson from the Ministerial Association and Christian Endeavor Convention (*The New York Times, *January 20, 2007, p. A25).*

617. **If you must hold yourself up to your children as an object lesson, hold yourself up as a warning and not as an example.**
—George Bernard Shaw

618. **His mother was a rigorous rationalist.**
—Writer D. T. Max, on Florence Noiville's book, A Life, *about Isaac Bashevis Singer, translated by Catherine Temerson.*

619. **"He has all the virtues I dislike and none of the vices I admire."**
—Sir Winston Churchill

620. **When I was a boy of 14, my father was so ignorant I could hardly stand to have the old man around. But when I got to be 21, I was astonished at how much the old man had learned in seven years.**
—Mark Twain

621. **Spend the day at home and you'll never remember it. Spend the day outdoors with me, and you'll never forget it.**
—Elizabeth Terwilliger, naturalist.

622. **DearDR.**
Ido not wemt to be a boy. I wemt to be a girl just my sisters.
Faem Stanley
—(family name omitted)

623. **"He is a self-made man and worships his creator."**
—John Bright

624. **The rights of the best of men are secured only as the rights of the vilest and most abhorrent are protected.**
—Chief Justice Charles Evans Hughes, 1927 (contributed by Sally Miller).

625. **"I have never killed a man, but I have read many obituaries with great pleasure."**
—*Clarence Darrow*

626. **"He can compress the most words into the smallest idea of any man I know."**
—*Abraham Lincoln, said of a colleague.*

627. **"I didn't attend the funeral, but I sent a nice letter saying I approved of it."**
—*Mark Twain*

628. **"I've just learned about his illness. Let's hope it's nothing trivial."**
—*Irvin S. Cobb*

629. **"They never open their mouths without subtracting from the sum of human knowledge."**
—*Thomas Brackett Reed*

630. **"In order to avoid being called a flirt, she always yielded easily."**
—*Charles, Count Talleyrand*

631. **Too much of a good thing is wonderful.**
—*Mae West*

632. **When a true genius appears in this world you will know him by this sign: - that the dunces are all in confederacy against him.**
—*Jonathan Swift*

633. **Anything worth doing is worth doing, imperfectly.**
—*Dr. Mark Wexman*

634. **Christianity is alright between consenting adults but should not be taught to children.**
—*Francis Crick, scientist.*

635. **Suddenly on this spring morning by the Oder, I remembered how in that iron winter of 1942, in a severe January snowstorm, on a night which was crimson from the flames of a village which Germans had set fire, a horse driver muffled in a sheepskin coat shouted suddenly, "Hey, comrades, where's the road to Berlin?"**

... I wonder if this joker, who had asked the way to Berlin near Balakleya, is still alive? And what about those who laughed at his question three years ago? And I wanted to shout to call to all our brothers, our soldiers, who are lying in the Russian, Ukrainian, Belorussian and Polish earth, who sleep forever on the fields of our battles: "Comrades, can you hear us? We've done it!"
—*A Writer at War: Vasily Grossman with the Red Army, 1941-1945,* *edited & translated by Antony Beevor & Luba Vinogradova, Pantheon.*

636. **Madam, I'm Adam - a palindrome.**
—*Random House College Dictionary, 1988, p. 957.*

637. **Misfortunes will happen to the wisest and best of men. Death will come, always out of season.**
—*Big Elk, Omaha tribe.*

638. **Let us put our minds together and see what life we can make for our children.**
 —*Sitting Bull, Lakota Sioux.*

639. **I believe God wants me to be president.**
—*George W. Bush*

640. **I welcome their hatred.**
 —*FDR, commenting on the plutocrats who considered him a class traitor.*

641. **Education is the key to the kingdom in America.**
—*Eugene M. Isenberg, CEO, Nabors Industries.*

642. **Their number is negligible, and they are stupid.**
—*Dwight D. Eisenhower, speaking about those who wanted to roll back the New Deal.*

643. **You were seeing things that God never intended you to see.**
—*Remains recovery worker at the World Trade Center site, after 9/11, NPR Interview.*

644. **If I have seen further it is by standing on the shoulders of Giants.**
—*Sir Isaac Newton*

645. **When [Stephen] Douglas invites any people, willing to have slavery, to establish it, he is blowing out the moral lights around us.**
—*Abraham Lincoln*

646. **Three centuries after [Sir Isaac] Newton, we're still learning our science one genius at a time.**
—*Peter Dizikes, "Twilight of the Idols," The New York Times Book Review, November 2, 2006, p. 31.*

647. **Old age is a shipwreck.**
—*Charles de Gaulle*

648. **The first casualty when war comes is truth.**
—*California Senator, Hiram Johnson, at the end of World War I.*

649. **Nobody can quite decide whether the Somme in 1916 was a victory or a defeat, because some things indeed do lie too deep for tears.**
—*Christopher Hitchens, The New York Times Book Review, January 28, 2007, p. 20, in a review of the book, "Dunkirk".*

650. **There's nothing more exhilarating than being shot at and missed!**
—*War correspondent Dexter Filkins, citing Sir Winston Churchill.*

651. **We should be inclined to say that what was characteristically paranoiac about the illness was the fact that the patient, as a means of warding off a homosexual wishful phantasy, reacted precisely with delusions of persecution of this kind.**

    These considerations therefore lend an added weight to the circumstance that we are in point of fact driven by experience to attribute to homosexual wishful phantasies an intimate (perhaps an invariable) relation to this particular form of disease. Distrusting my own experience on the subject, I have during the last few years joined with my friends C.G. Jung of Zurich and Sandor Ferenczi of Budapest in investigating upon this single point a number of cases of paranoid disorder which have come under observation. The patients whose histories provided the material for this enquiry included both men and women, and varied in race, occupation, and social standing. Yet we were astonished to find that in all of these cases a defence

against a homosexual wish was clearly recognizable at the very centre of the conflict which underlay the disease and that it was in an attempt to master an unconsciously reinforced current of homosexuality that they had all of them come to grief. This was certainly not what we had expected. Paranoia is precisely a disorder in which a sexual aetiology is by no means obvious; far from this, the strikingly prominent features in the causation of paranoia, especially among males, are social humiliations and slights. But if we go into the matter only a little more deeply, we shall be able to see that the really operative factor in these social injuries lies in the part played in them by the homosexual components of emotional life. So long as the individual is functioning normally and it is consequently impossible to see into the depths of his mental life, we may doubt whether his emotional relations to his neighbours in society have anything to do with sexuality, either actually or in their genesis. But delusions never fail to uncover these relations and to trace back the social feelings to their roots in a directly sensual erotic wish. So long as he was healthy, Dr. Schreber, too, whose delusions, culminating in a wishful phantasy of an unmis-takably homosexual nature, had, by all accounts, shown no signs of homosexuality in the ordinary sense of the word.
—*Notes on a Case of Paranoia, The Complete Psychological Works of Sigmund Freud, Volume XII, Hogarth Press, London, translated by James Strachey, p. 59.*

652. **The motives which predominate most human affairs are self-love and self-interest.**
—*George Washington*

653. **•I am a deeply religious nonbeliever. This is a somewhat new kind of religion.**
•Nature shows us only the tail of the lion. But I have no doubt that the lion belongs with it, even if he cannot reveal himself all at once. We see him only the way a louse that sits upon him would.
•Nationalism is an infantile disease, the measles of mankind.
•Newton, forgive me.
—*Albert Einstein, from Albert Einstein: His Life and Universe, Walter Isaacson, Simon & Schuster.*

654. **Making love is the friendliest thing two people can do.**
  —*Bruce Mainwaring [1953].*

655. **Women who fall in love with lifers are not really so hard to fathom. Convicts are a little like married men: trapped and grateful for whatever they can get.**
  —*Alessandra Stanley, commenting on "Women Who Love Bad Men," one of the episodes in the WE documentary series "Secret Lives of Women," in* The New York Times.

656. **"Heroes don't come home; survivors come home. But I thank you."**
  —*Reply by eighty-eight-year-old baseball Hall-of-Famer, Bob Feller, after being told by a baseball fan that he was also a hero because of his World War II naval service.*

657. **Hurbinek was a nobody, a child of death, a child of Auschwitz. He looked about three years old, no one knew anything of him, he could not speak and he had no name; that curious name, Hurbinek, had been given to him by us, perhaps by one of the women who had interpreted with those syllables one of the inarticulate sounds that the baby let out now and again. He was paralysed from the waist down, with atrophied legs, thin as sticks; but his eyes, lost in his triangular and wasted face, flashed terribly alive, full of demand, assertion, of the will to break loose, to shatter the tomb of his dumbness. The speech he lacked, which no one had bothered to teach him, the need of speech charged his stare with explosive urgency: it was a stare both savage and human, even mature, a judgement, which none of us could support, so heavy was it with force and anguish....**

  During the night we listened carefully: ...from Hurbinek's corner there occasionally came a sound, a word. It was not, admittedly, always exactly the same word, but it was certainly an articulated word; or better, several slightly different articulated words, experimental variations on a theme, on a root, perhaps on a name.

  Hurbinek, who was three years old and perhaps had been born in Auschwitz and had never seen a tree; Hurbinek, who had fought like a man, to the last breath, to gain his entry into the world of men, from which a bestial power had excluded him; Hurbinek, the nameless, whose tiny forearm - even his - bore the tattoo of Auschwitz; Hurbinek died in the first days of March

1945, free but not redeemed. Nothing remains of him: he bears witness through these words of mine.[34]
[34]*—Primo Levi, <u>The Reawakening</u>, pp. 25-26.*

658. **My life has become a little island of pain, floating on a sea of indifference.**
—Sigmund Freud, terminally ill from the oral cancer caused by his many years of cigar-smoking.

659. **WANTED: Men for hazardous journey, low wages, intense cold, long months of darkness and constant risks. Return uncertain.**
—Ad placed by the Antarctic explorer, Ernest Shackleton, in a London newspaper in 1913, in preparation for his ill-fated expedition of 1916.

660. **Murray Kempton once defined a great beauty as the woman no man was not better for having known.**
—Darryl Pinkney, writing in <u>The New York Review of Books</u> about the late NYRB editor, Barbara Epstein.

661. **It is well, I die hard, but I am not afraid to go.**
—George Washington, last words (December 14, 1799).

662. **My best friends solemnly regarded me as a madman, and my wife and family alone gave me encouragement.**
—John James Audubon

663. **You have sat too long here for any good you have been doing! Depart, I say, and let us have done with you! In the name of God, go!**
—A statement by MP Leo Amery, a backer of Sir Winston Churchill, addressed to Prime Minister Sir Neville Chamberlain in the British House of Commons on May 7, 1940, in protest of Chamberlain's policy of appeasement regarding Hitler's recent conquests in Europe. (From <u>The New York Times Book Review</u>, Sunday, April 29, 2007, p. 15).

664. **When two people make love, there are always four persons involved.**
—[the male and female in each person, paraphrasing Sigmund Freud].

665. **Priests dread the advance of science as witches do the approach of light.**
—Thomas Jefferson

666. **Fear no more the heat o' the sun,**
      Nor the furious winter's rages;
      Thou thy worldly task hast done,
      Home art gone, and ta'en thy wages;
      Golden lads and girls all must,
      As chimney-sweepers, come to dust.
      —*Shakespeare: Coriolanus – Sonnets, IV, ii, 258.*

667. **She [Sigmund Freud's mother] liked to call her son "my golden**
      Siggy"...
      —The Death of Sigmund Freud, *Mark Edmundson, Bloomsbury USA,*
      2007, p. 162.

668. **An aged man is but a paltry thing,**
      A tattered coat upon a stick, unless
      Soul clap its hands and sing, and louder sing,
      For every tatter in its mortal dress.
      —*Irish poet William Butler Yeats, [in] The Death of Sigmund Freud, Mark*
      Edmundson, Bloomsbury USA, 2007, p. 133.

669. **The daily reports flow in, in a kind of seamless syrup of insanity.**
      —*Simon Winchester, in The Professor and the Madman.*

670. **I went to bed that night in the lonely hotel room. I could not**
      sleep, and then, in the gray light between darkness and dawn,
      the words came to me line by line, stanza by stanza. I lay
      perfectly still, and the words came sweeping on with the rhythm
      of marching feet, pauseless, resistless. I saw the long line
      swinging into place before my eyes. I heard the voice of a na-
      tion speaking through my lips. Then when the last line was
      ended, I sprang from my bed and groping for pen and paper I
      scrawled in the gray twilight "The Battle Hymn of the Republic."
      —*Julia Ward Howe, as quoted in The New York Times, October 23, 2007,*
      p. D4.

671. **To the Editor:**

      Re "Shhh...My Child is Sleeping (In My Bed, Um, With Me"
      (Well, Oct. 23):
      Our daughter is now nearing 10 and I can only say that "co-
      sleeping" was the wisest decision my wife could have made. It
      saved her from sleep deprivation, which can be far more

damaging to a young family's life than whatever opinions the neighbors might express.

My wife chose to go with her instincts. She also chose her instincts when it came to breast-feeding. For both our children, co-sleeping meant long-term breast-feeding - our first child for three years and our son for four years. We believe that our children know we are there for them and we believe that co-sleeping has been an essential element in securing trust between us. Trust leads to understanding, which leads to peace and a good night's sleep for us all.

—*Michael Marnin Jacobs, Rovaniemi, Finland, The New York Times, October 30, 2007.*

672. **The most fortunate author is one who is able to say as an old man that all he had of life giving, invigorating, uplifting, enlightening thoughts and feelings still lives on in his writings, and that he himself is only the gray ash, while the fire has been rescued and carried forth everywhere.**

—*Friedrich Wilhelm Nietzsche, [in] The Death of Sigmund Freud, Mark Edmundson, Bloomsbury USA, New York, NY, 2007, p. 228.*

673. **He goes on to tell the story of a woman who, after her husband was fatally mauled by the dancing bear they had raised together, begged a visiting official for assistance: "'I have nothing sir, nothing at all - not even a roof for me and my animal.' 'Your animal? You mean the one that ate your husband?' 'Oh, sir, it's all I have left of the poor man.'"**

—*"The Discovery of France, A Historical Geography from the Revolution to the First World War," by Graham Robb. Illustrated. 454 pp. W. W. Norton & Company, in a review by Caroline Weber, The New York Times Book Review, November 4, 2007, p. 12.*

674. **When asked why she had consented to marry Mr. Stilwell, the 80-year-old Confederate Civil War veteran, when she herself had been only twenty, she answered, "I'd rather be an old man's darlin' than a young man's slave."**

—*The New York Times, August 29, 1997.*

675. **Be ashamed to die until you have won some victory for humanity.**

—*Horace Mann, first president of Antioch College, in Yellow Springs, Ohio (now the college motto).*

676. **"Memorial" – definition #3 - Something by which the memory of a person, thing or event is preserved, as a monumental erection.**
—*The Oxford English Dictionary*

677. **America is now "an insanely religious country."**
—*Harold Bloom*

678. **If you hear hoof beats, think horses, not zebras.**
—*SNN*

679. **Up to the age of sixty I thought it was a bone. (Jean Mounet-Sully – French actor and "a lion of a man")**
—*SNN*

680. **I am not a member of any organized party. I am a Democrat.**
—*Will Rogers, as quoted by Princeton professor Paul Krugman in his The New York Times column of January 26, 2007.*

681. **Curiosity is the root of the tree of knowledge.**
—*Charlotte Wolff, M.D., British psychiatrist.*

682. **Fewer still know of his fraught relationship with the government that now hallows his name:**

The same year that King proclaimed "I Have a Dream" from the steps of the Lincoln Memorial, J. Edgar Hoover's FBI - whose surveillance of King both Robert and John F. Kennedy approved - sent to King's home an audiotape of his love-making sounds with various paramours; an accompanying note urged him to commit suicide before his "filthy, abnormal fraudulent self is bared to the nation."
—*Joshua Jelly-Shapiro, in his review of the book "King - Pilgrimage to the Mountaintop," by Harvard Sitkoff, San Francisco Chronicle Book Review, January 20, 2008, Section M, p. 1.*

683. **From Native Tongue**
You go from us into a new becoming;
We rejoice for you and wish you an easy journey out into the light.
The winds will speak to us of you,
The waters will mention your name;
Snow and rain and fog, first light and last light, all will remind

Us that you had a certain way of being that was dear to us.
You go back to the land you came from and on beyond.
We will watch for you from time to time.
Amen
—*For Dan Bavosa, August 7, 1962 – November 20, 1995 and Joseph Daniel Crowley, July 16, 1990 – August 14, 2006.*

684. **Wagner's music is much better than it sounds.**
—*George Bernard Shaw, early in this career, working as a music critic [Courtesy of Richard Gale Matthews].*

685. **Look deep into nature, and then you will understand everything better.**
—*Albert Einstein*

686. **Poverty becomes a wise man as a red ribbon a white horse.**
—*Old Japanese saying.*

687. **If a nation expects to be ignorant and free, in a state of civilization, it expects what never was and never will be.**
—*Thomas Jefferson*

688. **All great truths begin as blasphemies.**
—*George Bernard Shaw (1856-1950).*

689. **Her voice was like "carved steam."**
—*A New York Times music reviewer, commenting on a performance by Feist, the Canadian folk-singer.*

690. **Give nature the tools, and get out of the way. Trust your crazy ideas.**
—*Dr. Doris A. Taylor, leader of the team reported to have successfully created a beating rat heart in a laboratory. "Team Creates Rat Heart Using Cells of Baby Rats," Lawrence K. Altman, The New York Times, January 14, 2008, p. A12.*

691. **The most beautiful makeup for a woman is passion. But cosmetics are easier to buy.**
—*Yves Saint Laurent*

692. **LOVE'S ILLOGIC**
      This bond called intimacy
      Thrives on broken boundaries,
      Lives in errant angles.
      Who really care where you
      End and I begin?
      Between lovers
      There exist no rigid rules
      As romance laughs at
      The seriousness of science,
      The rationale of physics.
      When we hold each other
      One plus one knows no two,
      As closeness ridicules
      The calculations of calculus,
      The logic of mathematics.
      And when night kisses dawn
      So do we, as we wink
      At the timelessness of time,
      Ignorant of any order,
      Only aware of one another.
      —*Roger Graner*

693. **Cloth napkins were whipped out for every meal. There was much serving of coffee and tea and even breakfast in bed, along with the morning newspaper and an insouciant smile. We were both losing weight despite drinking wine as if it were water and eating fat-laden foods. I put this down to the sex: appetite fans out and succumbs to carnal recreation.**
      —*Suzanne Finnamore, "When the Chutney's Gone, Modern Love," The New York Times, Sunday, April 6, 2008.*

694. **Nobody who writes faster can write better, and nobody better is faster.**
      —*A. J. Liebling, writer and critic, speaking of himself.*

695. **This blessed plot, this earth, this realm, this England.**
      —*Wm. Shakespeare, Richard II.*

696. **...though a living cannot be made at art, art makes life worth living. It makes starving, living.**
      —*John Sloane, English painter.*

697. **But complete sanity can only come through self-understanding. Unfortunately, many schizophrenic individuals do not want to have any awareness of the actual causes of their mental problems since such knowledge can be very painful. These individuals therefore cling to the medical model for much the same reason which had formerly induced them to cling to their delusional beliefs: to keep themselves from being aware of certain aspects of their personalities which they find thoroughly and dreadfully disturbing.**
—John Modrow, *How To Become A Schizophrenic - The Case Against Biological Psychiatry, Apollyon Press, Everett, Washington, 1992, p. 231.*

698. **JEALOUS IS POISON**
     GROCERY   PROP: G. MALUNGA
—*Name painted on front of grocery store in Nigeria.*

699. **Let's get the show on the road!**
—*Phyllis Ebbert Anderson, when informed she was dying from pancreatic cancer, as reported by her daughter, Tammy. [Contributed by Aileen Chivers, a close friend of the Anderson family].*

700. **P.S. Poor Eastham is gone at last. He died awhile before day this morning. They say he was very loath to die.**
     No clerk is appointed yet.
—*Abraham Lincoln, Letter No. 7, dated February 25, 1842, to his friend Joshua Speed, The Intimate World of Abraham Lincoln, C. A. Trip, Thunder's Mouth Press, New York, 2005, p. 265-266).*

701. **About the Scythians, for example, he said that they take the seeds of...cannabis, creep [into a tent-like structure], and throw the seeds onto the blazing-hot stones within. When the seeds hit the stones, they produce smoke and give off a vapor such as no steam bath in Hellas could surpass. The Scythians howl, awed and elated by the vapor. This takes the place of a bath for them, since they do not use any water at all to wash their bodies. Archaeology confirms this account in detail.**
—*"The Great Marathon Man, Peter Green," New York Review of Books, 5/15/2008, p. 33, quoting from* The Histories by Herodotus.

702. **I am not sure I need a coat.**
—*Dr. Martin Luther King's last words, replying to the suggestion he go back inside his Lorraine Motel room from the balcony to get one.*

703. **What wound did ever heal but by degrees.**
—Shakespeare's *Othello*

704. **I think it's saliva when it's inside your mouth and spit when it's outside your mouth.**
—One pre-teen girl to another, in discussing this weighty matter, overheard by Madeleine King and reported by Leah Garchik in her May 19, 2008 column in the *San Francisco Chronicle*.

705. **The ideal man bears the accidents of life with dignity and grace, making the best of circumstances.**
—Aristotle, 384-322 B.C.

706. **My husband and I have been married 15 years, and my heart still skips a beat when I see him.**
—Tina, as reported in a column by Dear Abby.

707. **Center my heart, boys. Don't mangle the body.**
—Last words of John D. Lee, Mormon militia leader, executed by a U.S. military firing squad in connection with the massacre of 120 settlers at Mountain Meadows in 1857.

708. **Much learning does not teach understanding.**
—Heraclitus, *On the Universe*.

709. **Si jeunesse savait, si veillesse pouvait (if youth knew, if the aged were able)**
—Old French saying, original SNN.

710. **I fired the gardener because he ate all my peaches.**
—Overheard by Alyssa Ghiringhelli, 11, (Leah Garchik column, *San Francisco Chronicle*, 7/24/2008).

711. **Emotional incest with the mother is indeed the very essence of lesbianism. [and likewise of male homosexuality – JMM].**
—Charlotte Wolff, M.D., *Love Between Women*, p. 60.

712. **That means nigger citizenship... Now, by God, I'll put him through. That is the last speech he will ever make.**
—John Wilkes Booth, commenting on the speech he had heard President Abraham Lincoln deliver in Washington, D.C., on April 11, 1865. Three days later Lincoln was dead.

713. **I'm always ready, sweetie.**
—Sam Manekshaw, a field marshal in the Indian Army, when asked by Prime Minister Indira Gandhi in 1971, prior to the start of the war with Pakistan, "General, are you ready for the war?" [Obituaries, The New York Times, 6/30/2008, page A-19].

714. **For where the flames of love arise**
Then Self, the gloomy tyrant dies.
—From the Ghazals of Muhammad ibn Muhammad (Jalal al-Din) Rumi, translated by Ruckert.

715. **While studying wild baboons in Kenya, I once stumbled upon an infant baboon huddled in the corner of a cage at the local research station. A colleague had rescued him after his mother was strangled by a poacher's snare. Although he was kept in a warm, dry spot and fed milk from an eyedropper, within a few hours his eyes had glazed over; he was cold to the touch and seemed barely alive. We concluded he was beyond help. Reluctant to let him die alone, I took his tiny body to bed with me. A few hours later I was awakened by a bright-eyed infant bouncing on my stomach. My colleague pronounced a miracle. "No," Harry Harlow would have said, "he just needed a little contact comfort."**
—Barbara Smuts, in The New York Review of Books, [date and page no. not recorded] in her review of "LOVE AT GOON PARK, "Harry Harlow and the Science of Affection," by Deborah Blum. Illustrated. 336 pp., Cambridge, Mass.: Perseus Publishing.

716. **At every crossing on the road that leads to the future, each progressive spirit is opposed by a thousand men appointed to guard the past.**
—Maurice Maeterlinck, courtesy of Joanna Wojewoda.

717. **We wanted to get married, and so we just thought, let's go there.**
—Anna-Bell, a 6-year-old German girl, on trying to elope to Africa with her 5-year-old boyfriend, stopped at railroad station by the police. (Time magazine, 1/19/09.).

718. **Man makes his end for himself out of himself: no end is imposed by external considerations, he must realize his true**

nature, must be what nature orders, so must discover what his nature is.
—From the _Nichomachean Ethics,_ dated 1877.

719. **All creation is a mine,
and every man a miner.**
—_Abraham Lincoln_

720. **Too old too soon/Too smart too late.**
—_Postcard drawing of an old cowboy, wistfully admiring all the pretty ladies in a saloon._

721. **For instance, it is quite certain that ever since water has been boiled in covered vessels, men have seen the lids of the vessels rise and fall a little, with a sort of fluttering motion, by force of the steam; but so long as this was not specially observed, and reflected, and experimented upon, it came to nothing. At length, however, after many thousand years, some man observes this long-known effect of hot water lifting a potlid, and begins a train of reflection upon it. He says, "Why, to be sure, the force that lifts the pot-lid will lift anything else, which is no heavier than the pot-lid. And, as man has much hard lifting to do, cannot this hot water power be made to help him?" He has become a little excited on the subject, and he fancies he hears a voice answering "Try me."**
—_Abraham Lincoln, from "Discoveries, Inventions and Improvements," a lecture by Mr. Lincoln from 1859._

722. **This is the true joy in life, the being used for a purpose recognized by yourself as a mighty one; the being thoroughly worn out before you are thrown on the scrap heap; the being a force of nature instead of a feverish selfish little clod of ailments and grievances complaining that the world will not devote itself to making you happy.**
—_George Bernard Shaw (1856-1950)._

723. **Thrice happy they, and more, whom an unbroken bond unites and whom love, unsevered by bitter quarrels, shall not release until the last day of all.**
—_Horace (65 - 8 B.C.)._

724. **It has often and confidently been asserted, that man's origin can never be known. But ignorance more frequently begets confidence than does knowledge: it is those who know little, and not those who know much, who so positively assert that this or that problem will never be solved by science.**
—*Charles Darwin, 1871.*

725. **...deeper into the engulfing indifference that readies us for death.**
—*John Updike, in The Widows of Eastwick.*

726. **It doesn't matter whom you love, or how you love, but that you love.**
—*Melinda Campi*

727. **You don't have intuition. You have paranoia.**
—*Woman overheard talking on cell phone. (Leah Garchik column, San Francisco Chronicle).*

728. **Curiosity did not kill this cat.**
—*Studs Terkel (1912-2008) (his preferred epitaph).*

729. **Oh! If you knew how much I sigh to see you.**
—*Marquis de Lafayette, in letter to loved one, 1777.*

730. **Life is so short that killing yourself is like falling out of an airplane without a parachute and then, on the way down, you blow your brains out.**
—*David Lozell Martin, writer and memoirist.*

731. **How extremely stupid not to have thought of that!**
—*Thomas Henry Huxley, on being first informed of his friend Charles Darwin's new theory of evolution.*

732. **The river now flowing by is not the same river that passed yesterday.**
—*Greek philosopher Heraclitus (c. 540 - c. 480 B.C.), reflecting on change.*

733. **To philosophize is to learn how to die.**
—*Cicero*

734. **I meet you in every dream.**
—*Alexander Hamilton, in letter to loved one, 1780.*

735. **His end has been all too tragic for his life. For once reality and his brains came into contact and the result was fatal.**
—*Thomas Henry Huxley, commenting on the death of Bishop Samuel Wilberforce, who publicly scorned Darwin's theory of evolution. (Wilberforce had been thrown head-first from his horse, fatally injuring him).*

736. **What can be more curious than that the hand of a man, formed for grasping, that of a mole for digging, the leg of a horse, the paddle of a porpoise, and the wing of a bat should all be constructed on the same pattern and should include the same bones in the same relative positions.**
—*Charles Darwin*

737. **Older lady in Springfield, IL - "You are the homeliest man I have ever seen."**
A. Lincoln - "I know, but what can I do?"
Older lady - "Well, You could stay home."

I leave it to you, my audience. If I were two-faced, would I be wearing this one?
—*Abraham Lincoln, in his debate with Stephen Douglas, 1858.*

738. **A coward dies a thousand deaths, a brave man only one.**
—*paraphrasing Shakespeare: Julius Caesar, II, ii, 32.*

739. **Revolutions are the "locomotives of history."**
—*Karl Marx*

740. **This war is eating my life out.**
—*Abraham Lincoln, Feb. 6, 1864.*

741. **I'm extremely happy with [Michelle], and part of it has to do with the fact that she is at once completely familiar to me, so that I can be myself and she knows me very well and I trust her completely, but at the same time she is also a complete mystery to me in some ways. And there are times when we are lying in bed and I look over and sort of have a start. Because I realize here is this other person who is separate and different and has different memories and backgrounds and thoughts and feelings.**

It's that tension between familiarity and mystery that make for something strong, because, even as you build a life of trust and comfort and mutual support, you retain some sense of surprise or wonder about the other person.
—Barack Obama, Mariana Cook interview, 26 May 1996, excerpted in "A Couple in Chicago," New Yorker, 19 January 2009. Obama and Michelle Robinson were married in October 1992.

742. **Never in the field of human conflict was so much owed by so many to so few.**
—Sir Winston Churchill, in Parliament, August 20, 1940, speaking of the valor of the Royal Air Force command in battling the hordes of German bombers and fighter planes attacking England.

743. **My mother did it.**
—Bookmaker Arnold "The Big Bankroll" Rothstein, when asked by the police shortly before he died to identify the person(s) who had shot him in a New York City hotel room, in 1928.

744. **The more I think about it, the more I realize there is nothing more artistic than to love others.**
—Vincent van Gogh

745. **During his [Judge Abner J. Mikva's] first year of law school at the University of Chicago, he walked into the storefront of an Eighth Ward committeeman to volunteer to work on the campaign of the Democratic reformers Adlai E. Stevenson and Paul Douglas. The committeeman, he recalled in an often-told story, took the fat cigar out of his mouth and asked gruffly, "Who sent you?"**

   "Nobody," the young Mr. Mikva replied.

   "We don't want nobody nobody sent," the committeeman growled.
—John Schwartz, The New York Times, June 26, 2010, p. A 14.

746. **You promised me that you would help me when I could no longer carry on. It is only torture now and it has no longer any sense.**
—Sigmund Freud, to his doctor Max Schur, asking him to end [by morphine injection] his suffering when he could no longer endure the intense agony caused by his jaw cancer - a request that was shortly thereafter fulfilled.

747. **Nobody wants you when you're old and grey there'll be some changes made.**
—*Dave Brubek, performing artist and jazz great.*

748. **But at my back I always hear/Time's winged chariot hurrying near.**
—*Andrew Marvell, 1621-1678, English poet.*

749. **Men Along The Shore*!***
—*the call that would go out along the New York City waterfront during colonial days when strong men were needed to unload the incoming cargo-laden Clipper ships. Hence the word "longshoreman".*

750. **COLCHAMIRO — Constance M. on September 8 of a broken heart. Beloved wife of the late Leon Colchamiro. [...]**
—*Obituary page, The New York Times, 9/10/2010.*

751. **Champagne for your real friends and real pain for your sham friends.**
—*the painter Francis Bacon's favorite Irish toast.*

752. **Even a broken clock is right twice a day.**
—*Robert H. Frank, The New York Times, Business, August 8, 2010, p. 7.*

753. **...a layman's document, not a lawyer's contract.**
—*Franklin Delano Roosevelt, 1882-1945, 32nd president of the U.S., 1933-1945, commenting on how he felt the U.S. Constitution should be regarded.*

754. **A revolution is not a dinner party.**
—*Mao Tse-tung, justifying the murder of landlords by peasants.*

755. **During one of his first sexual experiences the girl asked him, mortifyingly, "Should I have all that rammed up my guts?" "Yes," Golding stammered.**
—*Dwight Garner, The New York Times, July 7, 2010, p. C 6, referring to William Golding, British novelist and Nobel Prize winner (1983) in Literature.*

756.   **...the only man I ever saw who was a villain from the bark to the
       core.**
       —*John Randolph, foreman of the jury in the treason trial of Aaron Burr,
       speaking of American General James Wilkinson.*

757.   **...would be the greatest aid ever discovered to the happiness
       and security of individual families//— indeed, to mankind,
       because the greatest menace to world peace and decent stan-
       dards of life today is not atomic energy but sexual energy.**
       —*Dr. John Rock, in 1954, the lead researcher in the development of the
       oral contraceptive pill.*

758.   **...the Order of the boot.**
       —*what then-Prime Minister Sir Winston Churchill said he was presented
       with when his Conservative party lost the elections in 1945 to the Labour
       party, thus forcing him out of office.*

759.   **Refudiate, misunderestimate, wee-wee'd up. English is a living
       language. Shakespeare liked to coin new words too.**
       —*Sarah Palin, New Statesman, London, August 2, 2010, p. 24.*

760.   **...the rantings of a schizophrenic.**
       —*novelist Sebastian Faulk, commenting on the Quran. [the same could
       be said about the "bibles" of all religions - JMM].*

761.   **A human being is part of a whole, called by us universe, a part
       limited in time and space. He experiences himself, his thoughts
       and feelings as something separated from the rest ...a kind of
       optical delusion of his consciousness. This delusion is a kind of
       prison for us, restricting us to our personal desires and to
       affection for a few persons nearest to us. Our task must be to
       free ourselves from this prison by widening our circle of com-
       passion to embrace all living creatures and the whole of nature
       in its beauty.**
       —*Albert Einstein, 1879-1955, German physicist, U.S citizen from 1940,
       formulator of the theory of relativity.*

762.   **Over the phone I found her to be more caring, loving than any-
       one I had ever met - and genuinely nice all the time," he re-
       called. "She's everything good.**
       —*Former New York police detective Michael Fabozzi, speaking of his
       beloved Melinda Thomas, The New York Times, May 17, 2009, VOWS.*

763. **By the end, when the pilots overcame their obstacles and finally got up into the air to the swelling of music, tears welled up in my eyes right after I rolled them.**
—*Jason Zinoman, in his review of the play* Black Angels Over Tuskegee, *with its melodramatic ending. (*The New York Times, *2/18/2010, p. C 3.).*

764. **...though a little vain and silly, a bird of courage.**
—*Benjamin Franklin, commenting on the difference he perceived between the turkey and the bald eagle, the latter which he considered to be a bird of bad moral character.*

765. **[She is the] most interesting specimen in the whole series of vertebrate animals.**
—*Charles Darwin, speaking of his future wife, Emma Wedgwood, during their courtship.*

766. **...like a bag a doorknobs that wouldn't open any doors.**
—*the attorney for Maryann Burk Carver, wife of writer Raymond Carver, whom he was divorcing, commenting on what his client's post-divorce life would be like if she did not receive a decent court settlement.*

767. **[Criticism is] prejudice made plausible.**
—*H. L. Mencken*

768. **A good walk spoiled.**
—*Mark Twain's description of the game of golf.*

769. **...mentally dead people brought their corpses with them for a long visit.**
—*Mark Twain, speaking of dull and boring visitors, as quoted by his daughter, Susy.*

770. **A film is a ribbon of dreams.**
—*Orson Welles*

771. **[He was] deficient in those little links which make up the chain of woman's happiness.**
—*Mary Owens, commenting on her unsuccessful courtship by Abraham Lincoln when he was in his twenties.*

772. **A gigantic mistake.**
—Sigmund Freud, on being asked about his impressions of America after his first-and-last visit there, in 1909 (He did tour Coney Island).

773. **A study of the history of opinion is a necessary preliminary to the emancipation of the mind.**
—John Maynard Keynes, 1883-1946, English economist and writer.

774. **A vain man, a frightened man, a bigoted man or an angry man cannot laugh at himself or be laughed at; but the man who can laugh at himself or be laughed at has taken another step towards the perfect sanity, which brings peace on earth and goodwill to men.**
—San Francisco attorney Nat Schmulowitz (died 1966), creator of the "world's largest collection of humor" in the Schmulowitz Collection of Wit & Humor - at the San Francisco Public library.

775. **A mother's availability to her child is always affected by her relationship with her husband, and in pathology, her availability to the child may be incompatible with her availability to her husband. As we saw in the Jones case, if a man needs his wife as [his] mother, he will not tolerate her being the child's. Since, in general, people do not know that [isolation alone] can impair the mind, only tradition, as in tribal society, or love, as in our own, makes a parent available to an infant for the necessary length of time. A father interested only in himself—"available only to himself"—who thinks only of his own need, can compel a troubled mother to withdraw from her child. In my experience one of the most striking qualities of the mothers of autistic children is that they are not bizarre, and although their later* children may be troubled, they are far from psychotic. The relationship between husband and wife, however, was bad; and in all but the Wilson family, the relationship was miserable during the time when the child was becoming autistic. But I think that Mrs. Wilson concealed the reality of the relationship in the early days.**
—Jules Henry, Pathways To Madness, Random House, New York, 1965, 1971, p. 290.

776. **ALBANY - Sienna forward Ryan Rossiter is nothing if not self-aware. With a 6-foot-10, 235-pound frame that looks as if it**

could still use a few sandwiches, Rossiter has become a favorite target of opposing student sections on the road.
—*Pete Thamel, The New York Times, 3/8/2010, p. D4.*

777. **A poet is someone who stands outside in the rain hoping to be struck by lightning.**
—*James Dickey, poet.*

778. **A limit of time is fixed for thee.**
—*Marcus Aurelius (Volume II).*

779. **A terrifying aspect of the psychosis called primary infantile autism is its quietness: since the baby is conveniently quiet, since such babies are "good" babies, parents think everything is fine. Either the baby "was born quiet" or, though noisy and annoying at first, he stopped crying, just as the pediatrician said he would, when his crying was ignored. At two years the baby does not talk. Well, the parents are told, some babies are late talkers.**

    Sometimes the full horror is not perceived until a nursery school teacher says the child seems "retarded" and does not get on with other children. Deprived of social stimulation, the child has "obeyed" his parents' wishes—-he has grown indifferent to society. The wish that the child be quiet has become the magic jest – the child is quiet forever.
—*Jules Henry, Pathways To Madness, Random House, New York, 1965, 1971, p.289.*

780. **Afterwards, on becoming very intimate with Fitz-Roy [Captain of the HMS Beagle], I heard that I had run a very narrow risk of being rejected on account of the shape of my nose. He was an ardent disciple of Lavater, and was convinced that he could judge of a man's character by the outline of his features; and he doubted that anyone with my nose should possess sufficient energy and determination for the voyage. But I think he was afterwards well satisfied that my nose had spoken falsely.**
—*Charles Darwin, Autobiography.*

781. **A system could not well have been devised more studiously hostile to human happiness than marriage.**
—*Percy Bysshe Shelley, 1792-1822, English poet.*

782. **Addicts, active or otherwise, are narcissistic as a matter of course, stuck on the holy music of the self to the exclusion of almost everything else.**
—*David Carr, former crack addict and presently culture reporter at The Times, in his review of the book "PORTRAIT OF AN ADDICT AS A YOUNG MAN: A Memoir." By Bill Clegg. 222 pp. Little, Brown & Company (New York Times Book Review, Sunday, June 27, 2010, p. 11).*

783. **All flesh is grass and the/reality of love is there/wild flowers in the field/and all flesh blooms/no longer than a flower...**
—*David Rosenberg, A Literary Bible/An Original Translation, 680 pp., Counterpoint.*

784. **As a simple soldier, I learned to carry out orders.**
—*Heinrich Boere, a former member of the Nazi SS, on trial in Aachen, Germany, for war crimes (Newsweek, 12/21/2009).*

785. **Albert Einstein defined insanity as doing the same thing over and over again and expecting a different result.**
—*SNN*

❋

786. **All the wiggles are out.**
—*Janet Sinkewicz, elementary school principal, speaking of the salutary effect on her students' behavior when they began having recess prior to their lunch rather than after it (The New York Times, 1/26/10, p. D-1).*

787. **An appeaser is one who feeds a crocodile, hoping it will eat him last.**
—*Sir Winston Churchill*

788. **And so Nancy Makin of Grand Rapids, Mich., has a wonderful story to tell about her transformation from a 703-pound recluse into a slender, successful motivational speaker. ["How I Lost More Than a Quarter Ton and Gained a Life," By Nancy Makin, Dutton. 304 pages. $25.95.]**
—*Abigail Zuger, M.D., in "Health," The New York Times, June 29, 2010, p. D-5.*

789. **And then of course there's the Babe, who has a second-act cameo on his deathbed in which he says his only regret is that "maybe I didn't need to spend so much time with my family."**
—Ben Brantley, <u>The New York Times</u>, in his review of the musical comedy "Johnny Baseball," June 10, 2010, p. C3.

790. **Anger blows out the lamp of the mind.**
—Robert G. Ingersoll, a 19th-century orator.

791. **As a result, Voyager's most telling moments, he writes, were when it turned and looked backward, at the Earth and Moon, at Saturn's rings back lighted by the Sun, or at last the whole solar system with Earth as the famous pale blue dot. As of this writing, the Voyagers have each traveled more than 15 billion winding miles to the very edge of the solar system – and us with them, only to find ourselves metaphorically back home, and, as T.S. Eliot wrote, to know the place for the first time.**
—Dennis Oberbye, in his review of Stephen J. Pyne's book, "Voyager - Seeking Newer Worlds in the Third Great Age of Discovery," (<u>The New York Times Book Review</u>, Sunday, August 29, 2010, p. 21).

792. **Animals know more than we think, and think a great deal more than we know.**
—Irene M. Pepperberg, in her book <u>Alex & Me</u>, speaking of her 30-year bond and scientific collaboration with her African grey parrot .

793. **But a mother who is available (not a "quiet" mother), who finds it hard to stay away, will be there often, even without a peep from the baby. Science knows nothing about the quiet babies that have been born to supremely available mothers; because those babies are compelled to join the human race by the loving energy of their mothers, they never come to the attention of doctors or psychologists. Finally, even a noisy baby born to a quiet mother may become autistic, never become human, because he never got the necessary social stimulation. Mrs. Jones in this book and Mrs. Portman in my "Culture Against Man" are withdrawn mothers who do not go to their babies. In such situations the pediatric folklore advises against spoiling the child by too much attention, counsels the mother to teach the baby who is boss," diagnoses prolonged crying as mere "fussing," unworthy of concern, and explains that the baby is only "crying for attention." All this supports the mother+ who**

stays away from her baby. No other culture has invented so many excuses for keeping a mother away from her infant.
—Jules Henry, Pathways To Madness, Random House, New York, 1965, 1971, p. 288.

794. **As for the man who invented it all, he remains a mystery in the film, living out his days in sybaritic bliss.**
—Stephen Holden, in his film review of "Hugh Hefner: Playboy, Activist and Rebel," The New York Times, July 30, 2010, p. C12.

795. **At home my parents argued all the time - they hated each other - so I used to go into my bedroom and play with my gramophone records and listen to the radio. I was surrounded by music. I created my own little world.**
—Sir Elton John, "Parade", 2/21/2010, p. 4.

796. **Be not tedious in Discussion/make not many Digressions.**
—one of George Washington's "rules of civility".

797. **Beautiful, beautiful. Magnificent desolation.**
—Buzz Aldrin, the second Apollo 11 crewman to set foot on the moon, describing what he saw there.

798. **Before enlightenment, chop wood, carry water; after enlightenment, chop wood, carry water.**
—a Buddhist saying.

799. **Canon Lewis, sounding as analytical and academic as the couple, called marriage "a wonderful confinement" and a big risk. "The risk is failure, the risk is limiting yourself to one relationship," he whispered. "But you're also deepening yourself. Marriage is an ordeal. In ancient times an ordeal is what you went through to develop your own authentic self."**
—Lois Smith Brady, The New York Times, Vows, August 8, 2010, p. 11.

800. **Benedict [Pope Benedict XVI] says he leads a 'wounded and sinner' church.**
—The New York Times, April 18, 2010.

801. **But I believe that the windshield is bigger than the rearview mirror.**
      —*Former U.S. Senator Tom Daschle, on the saying which helps him get through difficult periods in his life.*

802. **Given the sheer torture of his physical existence, such an affirmation was testimony to Nietzsche's own gigantic will — [a will that transformed into madness paranoid schizophrenia - JMM] when he collapsed on a Turin sidewalk in January 1889, with delusions that he had become a world-creating god.**
      —*Francis Fukuyama, in his* The New York Times *book review, May 9, 2010, of "Friedrich Nietzsche - A Philosophical Biography," by Julian Young, Illustrated. 649 pp., Cambridge University Press.*

803. **But the Constitution is the rock upon which our nation rests. We must follow it not only when it is convenient, but when fear and danger beckon in a different direction. To do less would diminish us and undermine the foundation upon which we stand.**
      —*Judge Lewis A. Kaplan, United States District Court in Manhattan [NYC], October 7, 2010, disallowing testimony from a key witness in the first trial of a former Guantanamo detainee.*

804. **Charley, your proofreader is an idiot; & not only an idiot, but blind; & not only blind, but partly dead.**
      —*Mark Twain, in a diatribe to his publisher.*

805. **Death and the sun are not to be looked at steadily.**
      —*La Rochefoucauld, 1613-1680, French moralist and composer of epigrams and maxims.*

806. **Dark blond hair appeared very clearly in my windshield. I remember a kind of mechanical curiosity about why this was happening and what it might mean.**
      —*Darin Strauss, in his memoir "Half a Life" (McSweeney's Books, 208 pages), describing the accident during his senior year in high school where he collided with Celine Zilke, an 11th grader who was riding her bicycle, killing her.*

807. **Death ends a life, but it does not end a relationship.**
      —*Gene, the 40-year-old narrator, in the play, "I Never Sang for My Father".*

808. **COME ON SHORE AND WE WILL KILL AND EAT YOU ALL: A New Zealand Story.**
      —*Christina Thompson, (Bloomsbury, 15).*

809. **DEAR DIARY: (This is a true story; it took place in Sheepshead Bay this winter.) In Dunkin'Donuts this morning, an old lady wearing a tattered watch cap started speaking to no one in particular.**
        "I can't sleep at night. /I have pains in my chest all the/time.
        My leg hurts and my children/do not love me."/People waiting in line/hid in their cell phones, looked/away or stared straight ahead./"I don't know what to do./I don't know where to turn./My husband died two years ago on the 27th."/Everyone pretended she wasn't there./The girls behind the counter took the next customers./The line inched forward./At a side table, a beautiful young lady with matching purple scarf and hat/looked at the old woman and said, simply,/"Honey, please sit down with me,/and your story."/It's possible, you see, /for one person to save the world.
      —*Mel Glenn, "Metropolitan Diary," <u>The New York Times</u>, March 2, 2009.*

810. **Dear posterity, if you have not become more just, more peaceful, and generally more rational than we are (or were) - why then, the Devil take you. Having, with all respect, given utterance to this pious wish, I am (or was) yours, Albert Einstein.**
      —*from a time capsule placed in 1936.*

❊

811. **Death is the most convenient time to tax rich people.**
      —*David Lloyd George, British Prime Minister, 1916-1922.*

812. **I would call him a person who has trouble adjusting to authority. He does not like his word to be questioned... I'm not totally surprised because we all felt like he might have, you know, a little problem between East and West - a mental problem.**
      —*Terrence N. Taylor, former father-in-law of Jason Rodriguez, who killed one and wounded five in a Florida office [Jennifer Steinhauer, <u>The New York Times</u>, November 7, 2009, p. A9].*

813. **English frock coats... little preventive bags invented by the English to save the fair sex from anxiety.**
—*Giovanni Jacopo Casanova (1725-1798), Italian adventurer and writer, referring to early condom-like devices.*

814. **Democracy is "a form of worship. It is the worship of jackals by jack-asses."**
—*H(Henry) L(Louis) Mencken, 1880-1956, U.S. Editor.*

815. **The birth of Ayumu and two other babies at the Primate Research Institute [Japan] in a five-month span in 2000 gave Matsuzawa the opportunity to observe mother-infant pairs intensely. The scientists learned that new mothers looked into the eyes of their babies 22 times per hour. And chimp babies, like human infants, communicate by imitation, sticking out their tongues or opening their mouths in response to similar adult human gestures.**
—*John Cohen, "Thinking Like a Chimpanzee," <u>Smithsonian</u>, September 2010, pp. 56-7.*

816. **Do what thy manhood bids thee do. From none but the self expect applause; He noblest lives and noblest dies who makes and keeps his self-made laws.**
—*Sir Richard Francis Burton, English explorer and diplomat.*

817. **Especially important was a startling communication from a clover blossom one summer day when I was about 14. It said, with utmost simplicity, 'I am.'"**
—*Mary Daly, 1928-2009, feminist theologian, in an essay in the New Yorker magazine in 1996.*

818. ***Fabulous sex was high on Bernard's menu even in the straitlaced 1910's.**
—*Robert Love's entertaining biography, "The Great Oom," depicts a bold and successful liar who could tell his gullible disciples with a straight face that oral sex, punishable in 1915 by up to 20 years in prison, was a sacred practice in India and produced orgasms 10 times longer than ordinary intercourse, Pankaj Mishra, in his review of "The Subtle Body - The story of Yoga in America", by Stefanie Syman, <u>The New York Times Book Review</u>, Sunday, July 25, 2010, p. 12.*

819. **Down with bad government and death to the gachupines! [— a disparaging term for Mexico's Spanish rulers.]**
    —*Father Miguel Hidalgo, in his famous "Grito de la Independencia" cry on September 16, 1810, the day long-celebrated as the beginning of Mexico's War of Independence from Spain (1810-1821), following three centuries of Spanish* colonial *domination.*

820. **Do what you love.**
    —*Don Fisher (1928-2009), Gap Inc. founder.*

821. **Don't believe everything you think.**
    —*automobile bumper sticker, contributed by Melinda Campi.*

822. **Dying man couldn't make up his mind which place to go — both have their advantages, "heaven for climate, hell for company."**
    —*Mark Twain*

823. **Either that wallpaper goes, or I do.**
    —*Oscar Wilde (1854-1900), Irish writer and wit, on his deathbed in a garishly-decorated hotel room.*

❋

824. **Everyone thought he was capable of being emperor, until he became it.**
    —*Tacitus, Roman historian (c55-c120 A.D.), writing about the Roman emperor, Galba.*

825. **Even a self-respecting hoodlum hasn't any use for that kind of fella. He buys them like he'd buy any other article necessary to this trade. But he hates them in his heart.**
    —*Al Capone, speaking about officials and others he had bribed.*

826. **Even if the world were perfect, it wouldn't be.**
    —*Lorenzo Pietro Berra (Yogi Berra, Yankee great)*

827. **Everyone takes the limits of his own vision for the limits of the world.**
    —*Schopenhauer, Arthur, 1788-1860, German philosopher.*

828. **Far-called, our navies melt away;//On dunes and headlands sinks the/fire;/Lo, all our pomp of yesterday/is one with Nineveh and Tyre!**
—*Rudyard Kipling, in his elegy to the British empire, marking Queen Victoria's Diamond Jubilee, in 1897.*

829. **Everybody has the same energy potential. The average person wastes his in a dozen little ways. I bring mine to bear on one thing only: my painting, and everything else is sacrificed to it –- you and everyone else, myself included.**
—*Pablo Picasso, 1881-1973, Spanish painter and sculptor in France.*

830. **Go to the bathroom mirror, look yourself in the mirror and say, "You're dying." It's not easy.**
—*Dr. Nicholas Christakis, commenting on how difficult it is for doctors to tell patients they are dying – The New York Times, 8/20/2009.*

831. **Everybody needs beauty as well as bread, places to play in and pray in, where Nature may heal and cheer and give strength to body and soul alike.**
—*John Muir, American naturalist.*

832. **Fame is like a river that beareth up things light and swollen and drowns things weighty and solid.**
—*Francis Bacon*

833. **For me the Arab-Jewish struggle is a tragedy. The essence of tragedy is the struggle of right against right... When evil men do evil, their deeds belong to the realm of pathology. But when good men do evil, we confront the essence of human tragedy.**
—*I.F. "Izzy" Stone, American journalist and publisher, I.F. Stone's Weekly.*

834. **Good fortune will elevate even petty minds, and give them the appearance of a certain greatness and stateliness, as from their high place they look down upon the world; but the truly noble and resolved spirit raises itself, and becomes more conspicuous in times of disaster and ill fortune.**
—*Plutarch, Greek biographer, A.D. c46-c120.*

835. **He had a kind of vitality that — I had never met anyone like that — that kind of rearranged my molecules.**
—*Ken Burns, American documentarian, speaking of his friend William Segal, 1905-2000, painter and spiritual teacher.*

836. **Everybody's got a hungry heart.**
—*Bruce "Boss" Springsteen*

837. **Favourite virtue: Simplicity, Idea of happiness: To fight, Favourite hero, Spartacus.**
—*Karl Marx, in Francis Wheen's 1999 biography Karl Marx.*

838. **First in war, first in peace, and first in the hearts of his fellow citizens.**
—*John Marshall/George Washington, The Life of George Washington, 1805-1807.*

839. **History will be kind to me for I intend to write it.**
—*Sir Winston (Leonard Spencer) Churchill, 1874-1965, British Prime Minister 1940-1945, 1951-1955, Nobel Prize for literature 1953.*

840. **Gender is between your ears, not between your legs.**
—*Chaz Bono, transgendered from a female to a male.*

841. **For I have sworn thee fair, and thought thee bright/ Who art as black as hell, as dark as night.**
—*William Shakespeare, Sonnet 147.*

842. **For me, life began with a one-night stand.**
—*Mary Pols, author of Accidentally on Purpose: The True Tale of a Happy Single Mother.*

843. **Genius is the unmastered personality.**
—*Christian Gauss, Dean of Princeton University, 1925-45.*

844. **He is in very much the same position as myself. He has to put matters in such a way as to make people who would otherwise hang him believe he is joking.**
—*George Bernard Shaw, referring to Mark Twain during the latter's visit to England in 1907.*

845. **Go into the world and do well. But more importantly, go into the world and do good.**
—*Minor Myers, Jr.*

846. **He socialized mainly with men he knew and women he knew not at all.**
—*Solomon Moore, describing a certain "prosperous" California business-man, The New York Times, 12/9/2009, p. A1.*

847. **He's a heart,**
He's an acorn from an oak tree,
He's young.
Kiss him!
—*penned by an unknown Irish scribe.*

848. **How sharper than a serpent's tooth it is to have a thankless child.**
—*Shakespeare's King Lear.*

849. **I am willing to love all mankind, except an American.**
—*Samuel Johnson ("Dr. Johnson"), 1709-1784, English lexicographer and writer.*

850. **I could not believe that the president of the United States had come down to the city of New Orleans and basically put up a stage prop... They put them up and the minute we are gone they took them down... It was an empty spot with one little crane. It was the saddest thing I have ever seen in my life. At that moment I knew what was going on and I've been a changed woman ever since.**
—*Senator Mary Landrieu, Democrat of Louisiana, describing her feelings after a fly-over of the Hurricane Katrina-breached 17th Street Canal in New Orleans, the day after she had already visited the site accompanied by President George W. Bush and numerous local dignitaries.*

851. **If it bleeds, it leads.**
—*old newspaper maxim.*

852. **I still cannot be in a car, headed for the Capitol, especially in the evening, and glimpse it in the distance without the hair**

standing up on my arms... **If ever that sight does not move me, I will know it is time to step aside.**
—*Senator Edward M. Kennedy, in True Compass: a Memoir.*

853. **He wanted sincerely to look after the little fellow who had no pull, and that's what a president is supposed to do.**
—*Harry S. Truman, U.S. President (1945-53), speaking about Andrew Jackson, U.S. President (1829-37).*

854. **He was a go-fast and turn-tight type guy.**
—*Bill Baker, describing his late friend Charles D. King, 82, a British engineer who led the team that developed the Range Rover vehicle. (The New York Times obituary, July 4, 2010, by Christopher Maag).*

855. **History is like a horse that gallops past your window and the true test of statesmanship is to jump from that window onto the horse.**
—*Shimon Peres, Prime Minister of Israel, 1984-86: Nobel peace prize 1994 – referring to the ongoing Israeli/Palestinian negotiations.*

856. **I am a radical myself, progressive, liberal to the core. But I do not want to be thrown over by a lot of demagogues, nincompoops, and shallow shouters.**
—*Joseph Pulitzer, 1847-1911, U.S. publisher and journalist.*

857. **Human nature, in no form of it, could ever bear prosperity.**
—*John Adams, writing to Thomas Jefferson, cautioning about the coming corruption of the country.*

858. **I paint as a means to make life bearable. Don't weep. What I have done is best for all of us. No use. I shall never be rid of this depression.**
—*Vincent Van Gogh, in a letter penned in 1890 just before fatally shooting himself in the chest, and after having earlier cut off his left earlobe.*

859. **How do you know whether a guy is worth staying with, or if you're on a slowly sinking ship?**
—*a request for advice sent to Amy Alkon, Advice Goddess, in the Marin County, CA, weekly – The Pacific Sun, 5/28 - 6/3, 2010.*

860. **I am sorry. It's a little word, I know. But it is true.**
—*Jason Getsy's last words before his execution on 8/18/09 in Lucasville, Ohio, for the murder of Ann Serafino, mother of Charles Serafino, the intended victim in a contract killing, who was wounded.*

861. **Hope is the basic ingredient of all vitality.**
—*Erik Erickson, psychoanalyst.*

862. **I b'leve I'll go wid de ole man.**
—*Shields Green, an escaped South Carolina slave, when asked by Frederick Douglass if he wanted to leave the meeting with him after Douglass had failed to dissuade John Brown from embarking on his ill-fated raid on Harper's Ferry in 1850 [courtesy of Herb Boyd, New York City, in Smithsonian magazine, December, 2009, p. 4].*

863. **I couldn't leave for the same reason people couldn't leave a marriage that had died a long time ago: Because all this couldn't have been in vain.**
—*Rachel Shukert, "Everything Is Going To Be Great - An Underfunded and Overexposed European Grand Tour," 312 pp. Harper Perennial.*

864. **I have heard him [Abraham Lincoln] say over and over again about sexual contact. 'It is the harp of a thousand strings.'**
—*Henry C. Whitney to William H. Herndon, June 23, 1887.*

865. **I have called this principle, by which each slight variation, if useful, is preserved, by the term Natural Selection.**
—*Charles Darwin, On the Origin of Species, Ch. 3.*

866. **I hope he was hurting. I hope it killed him...//You know, not only winning the game makes you feel good, but just knowing the other guy's suffering. And you know he was.**
—*Larry Bird, commenting on his rival, Magic Johnson, after Bird's Boston Celtics won the NBA championship against Johnson's Los Angeles Lakers in 1984 - in the HBO documentary "Magic & Bird: A courtship of Rivals".*

867. **I made my money the old-fashioned way. I inherited it.**
—*John Raese, West Virginia's Republican candidate for the U.S. Senate, as told to an interviewer in October, 2010.*

868. **I did not know that she could go away and take our lives with her, yet leave our dull bodies behind.**
—*Mark Twain, in a letter expressing his grief at the death of his beloved daughter, Susy, at age 24.*

869. **I die happy.**
—*Charles James Fox, British parliamentarian, whose long fight to abolish the slave trade ended in victory in 1806, several months before his death.*

870. **I hate war, as only a soldier who has lived it can, as one who has seen its brutality, its futility, its stupidity.**
—*Dwight David Eisenhower, U.S. general and president.*

871. **I have the blood of Africa within me.**
—*Barack Hussein Obama, in a speech to the people of Ghana, July, 2009.*

872. **I live with the puzzle of wondering how something so apparently crazy can be so captivating to millions of other members of my species.**
—*Diarmaid MacCulloch, professor of the history of the church at Oxford University, in his book Christianity: The First Three Thousand Years.*

873. **I never in my life felt more certain that I was doing right than I do in signing this paper. [If] my name ever goes into history it will be for this act, and my whole soul is in it.**
—*Abraham Lincoln, spoken to friends who were witness to his signing of the Emancipation Proclamation on January 1, 1863.*

874. **I have heard people say that you should never marry a man who does not love his mother.**
—*Artis Henderson, The New York Times, Modern Love, August 8, 2010, p. 8.*

875. **I think people should know that you derive the greatest satisfaction from serving others rather than serving yourself... I would want more and more Nigerians to define themselves also in this light of service to the nation and service to humanity.**
—*Umaru Musa Yar'Adua, President of Nigeria – May, 2007 until his death at age 58, May 5, 2010.*

876. **I started at the top and worked my way down.**
      —*Orson Welles, 1915-1985, U.S actor, director and producer.*

877. **I regret that I cannot accede to your request, because I should very much like to remain in the darkness of not having been analyzed.**
      —*Albert Einstein, in response to the suggestion that he undergo psychoanalysis, 1927.*

878. **I made Peter Pan by rubbing the five of you violently together, as savages with two sticks produce a flame.**
      —*J. M. Barrie, referring to the five sons of Mr. and Mrs. Arthur Llewelyn, in the dedication to the first published edition of his play, "Peter Pan".*

879. **I like pigs. Dogs look up to us. Cats look down on us. Pigs treat us as equals.**
      —*Sir Winston Churchill*

880. **I violate the Prohibition law – sure. Who doesn't?**
      The only difference is, I take more chances than the man who drinks a cocktail before dinner and a flock of highballs after it.
      —*Al(phonse) "Scarface" Capone, 1899-1947, U.S. gangster and Prohibition-era bootlegger, "Public Enemy No. 1".*

881. **I stay away from candy bars. They're full of transgendered fats.**
      —*Woman with dog tied to the workout equipment, "Fit Lite Gym in San Franciso," overheard by David Bye (Leah Garchik column, <u>San Francisco Chronicle</u>, 4/3/2009).*

882. **I would be scared if I thought you had the guts to do it.**
      —*Mother to suicidal daughter, when asked by the latter, "Should I slit my throat?"*

883. **If all the people who lived together were in love, the earth would shine like the sun.**
      —*Baptiste, in <u>Les Enfant du Paradis</u>.*

884. **I was shouting, but no one could hear me.**
      —*Rom Houben, a Belgian man, mistakenly believed to have been in a coma for 23 years following a car accident which had left him paralyzed.*

885. **If the law supposes that, the law is a ass, a idiot.**
—*Beadle Bumble, in Charles Dicken's* Oliver Twist.

886. **I was staying in the home of my father's mother in Jeddah. I had been sound asleep and was woken by my uncle yelling: "Look what your father has done!" I went into the sitting area and my family were gathered around the television. I soon learned that America was under attack. It was a very sad day.**
—*Omar bin Laden, son of Osama, speaking to British journalist Anastasia Taylor-Lind, about the events of September 11, 2001 (*New Statesman, *London, p. 26, 23 November 2009).*

887. **My father could be very kindly and he was very close to his mother. I remember his face glowing with happiness when he was with her.**
—*Omar bin Laden (ibid, see preceding quotation).*

888. **I thought you would rather have a live donkey that a dead lion.**
—*Ernest Shackleton, famed English explorer, explaining to his wife why he turned back only 97 miles from the South Pole during his 1909 Antarctic expedition.*

889. **If there is no struggle, there is no progress.**
—*Frederick Douglass, 1817-95, U.S. abolitionist.*

890. **I wish it was different, but it isn't. So you endure it.**
—*George Burgess, 96, who lives alone near Torrington, Wyoming,* The New York Times, *Quotation of the Day, 12/10/2009.*

891. **I wish that all were as I myself am. But each has a particular gift from God, one having one kind and another a different kind.**
—*St. Paul, 1 Corinthians 7, expressing his wish that all Christians could remain, like he had, single and celibate.*

892. **I would like the firing squad, please.**
—*Ronnie Lee Gardner, a condemned murderer in Utah, picking his method of execution (*The New York Times, *Quotation of the Day, 4/24/2010).*

893. **I used to smoke cigarettes/like a whore on a five-minute break.**
—*Carlos Carrea*

894. **In much wisdom is much grief.**
      —*Ecclesiastes*

895. **I was so scared that pilot and me was like husband and wife until we landed.**
      —*Baseball great Leroy (Satchel) Paige, commenting on his fear of flying, in Larry Tye's book "Satchel - The Life and Times of An American Legend," <u>The New York Times</u>, 6/14/2000.*

896. **I wonder by my troth, what thou and I Did, till we loved?**
      —*John Donne, 1573-1631, English poet and clergyman.*

897. **If you have seen the present then you have seen everything - as it has been since the beginning, as it will be forever. The same substance, the same form. All of it.**
      —*Marcus Aurelius, second-century A.D. Roman Emperor and scholar, in his <u>Meditations.</u>*

898. **I would wish people to live without superstition, to govern their lives with reason, and to conduct their relationships on reflective principles about what we owe one another as fellow voyagers through the human predicament - with kindness and generosity wherever possible, and justice always. None of this requires religion or the empty name of "god". Indeed, once this detritus of our ignorant past has been cleared away, we might see more clearly the nature of good, and pursue it aright at last.**
      —*A. C. Grayling, professor of philosophy, Birbeck College, University of London.*

899. **If we can no longer believe in forgiving sins, we might as well close the whole store.**
      —*Rupert Frania, the priest in charge of the congregation in Bad Tölz, Germany, speaking of the convicted pedophile, the Rev. Peter Hullerman, who had spent the last year and a half there (<u>The New York Times</u>, 3/16/2010, p. A 6).*

900. **It is difficult to imagine anything more terrifying than for an officer to become landed with a woman agent who suffers from an overdose of sex.**
      —*Maxwell Knight, an English MI-5 intelligence officer during World War II, in an internal memo to his fellow-officers. (<u>Defend The Realm, The Authorized History of MI-5</u>, by Christopher Andrews).*

901. **If I could get my brother in a fight with somebody his age, I was happy as hell, 'cause I liked to see him get beat up. [Said with a smile.]**
—*Larry Bird, in the HBO documentary "Magic & Bird: A Courtship of Rivals".*

902. **I'm not afraid of your camera. You think you're God, don't you, white man?**
—*Told to PBS "Frontline" reporter Martin Smith by a "bloody, dying man, possibly a looter," lying bound by his feet "and his face covered with flies" outside a Haitian police station following the 2010 earthquake (Mike Hale, Television Review, "The Quake", The New York Times, 3/30/2010).*

903. **If my fellow citizens want to go to hell, I will help them. It's my job.**
—*Supreme Court Justice Oliver Wendell Holmes, the "Great Dissenter," 1831-1935, U.S. jurist, here pungently distilling his theory of "judicial restraint" .*

904. **If I wasn't an actor, I think I would have gone mad.**
—*Laurence Olivier*

905. **If we are all born equal, why are some of us only cowboys?**
—*the first sentence in Muck, a memoir by Craig Sherborne.*

906. **It has been said that if you remember the '60's, you weren't there.**
—*Anonymous*

907. **If you have a sapling in your hand and they say to you, The Messiah has come, finish planting the sapling, then receive him.**
—*Jonathan ben Zakkai, first century rabbi.*

908. **I'm disappointed they didn't have the esophagus.**
—*Woman at the M. H. de Young Memorial Museum in San Francisco, discussing the Tut show, overheard by Ken Maley (Leah Garchik column, San Francisco Chronicle, 10/12/2009).*

909. **In sooth all gods I hate. 'Tis better to be bound on a rock than bound to the service of Zeus.**
—*Aeschylus (525-456 B.C.)*

910. **In the fields of observation chance favors only the prepared mind.**
—*Louis Pasteur, Inaugural lecture, University of Lille, December 7, 1854.*

911. **I'm not paying $7 a pound when it's just our low-level friends.**
—*Man to woman, while shopping at a Whole Foods market in San Francisco, overheard by Paul Wiefels [Leah Garchik column, San Francisco Chronicle, 10/9/2009].*

912. **It may come as a surprise to some to learn that George Washington had a delicate nervous system that behaved badly under certain types of stress. He could walk placidly through a hail of gunfire and go back to a happy dinner. But receiving a complaining letter from his troublesome mother, and having to sit and write her a response that explained why she should not consider moving to Mount Vernon, invariably gave him shoulder pains bad enough to force him to bed. Martha had observed this so many times that she ordered his bed prepared whenever an envelope from his mother appeared.**
—*Charles A. Cerami, Dinner at Mr. Jefferson's.*

913. **In our adversary system of criminal justice, any person hauled into court, who is too poor to hire a lawyer, cannot be assured a fair trial unless counsel is provided for him.**
—*Justice Hugo L. Black, writing for the Supreme Court in "Gideon v. Wainwright," 1963.*

914. **It is easier to build strong children than to repair broken men. [and women - JMM]**
—*Frederick Douglass, 1817-1895, U.S. abolitionist.*

915. **It is the writer's duty to tell the terrible truth, and it is a reader's civic duty to learn this truth.**
—*Vasily Grossman, in "The Hell of Treblinka," published in November, 1944, in the Soviet magazine Znamya. (The Red Army, accompanied by Grossman, had reached Treblinka in August, 1944).*

916. **Is it so critical to the future of grizzly bears as a world species if the North Cascades [Washington State] fades away?... Just asking that makes my teeth hurt.**
—*Doug Zimmer, a spokesman for the Fish and Wildlife service.*

917. **It is difficult to get a man to understand something when his salary depends on his not understanding it.**
—Upton Sinclair, 1878-1968, American novelist and reformer.

918. **In youth we learn; in age we understand.**
—Marie Ebner von Eschenbach

919. **It is in fact nothing short of a miracle that modern methods of instruction have not strangled the holy curiosity of inquiry.**
—Albert Einstein

920. **It is like taking a poor lamb to be sacrificed.**
—Queen Victoria, who had experienced nine pregnancies herself during her marriage to Prince Albert, weepingly commenting on the occasion of their oldest daughter's nuptials.

921. **It is with books as it is with men - a very small number play a great part.**
—Voltaire (Francois Marie Arouet), 1694-1778, French writer and philosopher.

922. **It is the duty of a newspaper to comfort the afflicted and afflict the comfortable.**
—H. L. Mencken

923. **It is, sir, as I have said, a small college. And yet there are those who love it.**
—Daniel Webster, arguing on behalf of Dartmouth College before the U.S. Supreme Court, March 10, 1818.

924. **I've never heard a bad thing about [name deleted]. I've never heard a good thing about [name deleted]. It's a total vacuum.**
—One union official, commenting on the death of the former union chief of another New York City union.

925. **Landau [Felix] did save Schulz for more than a year, until November 1942, by providing him with work and the means for minimal sustenance. Schulz, whose literary reputation as a short-story writer had already been established, had obtained false Aryan papers and was about to escape when another Gestapo sergeant, Karl Gunter, angry that Landau had killed his**

Jewish dentist, put a bullet in Schulz's head. He is said to have told Landau: "You killed my Jew. Now I've killed yours."
—*The New York Times* article.

926. **It seems there is a sort of calamity built into the texture of life.**
—*Frank Kermode*

927. **It was, as Wellington said of Waterloo, a close-run thing: a world religion founded on the brief public ministry, trial and execution of a single jew in a remote corner of the Roman Empire.**
—*Jon Meacham, editor of "Newsweek," in a book review in* The New York Times*, April 4, 2010.*

928. **It's not that I'm so smart. It's that you're so dumb.**
—*Admiral Hyman George Rickover, 1900-1986, considered the father of the nuclear navy, at the start of an interview with TV luminary Diane Sawyer, who had just complimented him on being so brilliant.*

929. **Last year's Belmont was like swallowing a spoon sideways.**
—*Jockey Kent Desormeaux, winner of this year's Belmont Stakes, commenting on his loss in 2008 aboard the favored Big Brown. [*The New York Times*, 6/7/2009].*

930. **Liberty is "the right to define one's own concept of existence, of meaning, of the universe and of the mystery of human life."**
—*Anthony Kennedy, Supreme Court Justice, in "Planned Parenthood v. Casey".*

931. **Jeden das Seine ["to each his own"]**
—*Sign at the entrance to Buchenwald concentration camp, where Jews, Gypsies, homosexuals and others were brought to be worked to death.*

932. **Mathematics is a way of thinking in everyday life. It is important not to separate mathematics from life.//You can explain fractions even to heavy drinkers. If you ask them, "Which is larger, 2/3 or 3/5?" it is likely they will not know. But if you ask, "Which is better, two bottles of vodka for three**

people, or three bottles of vodka for five people?" they will answer you immediately. They will say two for three, of course.
—Dr. Israel M. Gelfand (1913-2009), world-renowned Russian mathematician and professor of mathematics at Rutgers University [Obituaries, The New York Times, 10/8/2009].

933. **Killing seems to me a very unnatural trade, but these people are beyond nature as well as reason.//They might at this moment have peace and happiness, but they insist upon having their brains knocked out first.**
—Henry Strachey, secretary to General William Howe and Admiral Richard Howe, brothers who served as the commanders-in-chief of the British army and naval forces in the American colonies prior to 1778, in a letter home to his wife after the British had won the Battle of Long Island in August, 1776.

934. **Maybe all any of us wants is to feel singled out for some long, sweet, quenching draft of love, some open-throated guzzling of it - like what a baby gets at the breast.**
—Mary Karr, Lit: A Memoir, Harper, 386 pp.

935. **Just because the shades are up, doesn't mean you can go in.**
—courtesy of Martha Kyles.

936. **Let us never negotiate out of fear, but let us never fear to negotiate.**
—President John F. Kennedy

937. **Leave the matter of religion to the family altar, the church, and the private school, supported entirely by private contributions. Keep the church and the State forever separate.**
—Ulysses S. Grant, in a speech at Des Moines, Iowa, 1875.

938. **Let him who desires peace prepare for war.**
—Vegetius, a Roman writer of the fourth Century AD.

939. **Oh, my God. Grandma is texting!**
—woman looking at cell phone, talking to teenager, overheard at the Alameda County Fair by Elizabeth Fox (Leah Garchik column, San Francisco Chronicle, 9/21/2009).

940. **Kiss the hand you cannot bite.**
—A Romanian proverb.

941. **Let unconquerable gladness dwell.**
—the motto F.D.R. kept in his office.

942. **Love thou the rose, yet leave it on its stem.**
—Edward G. Bulwer-Lytton

943. **Life lures us with small favors to commit great crimes   [Note: Pls center this line, and there is no period after "crimes"]**
—Jules Henry

944. **Longing makes us who we are, makes us better than who we are, because longing fills the heart.**
—Andre Aciman, in Eight White Nights, Farrar, Straus & Giroux, 370 pp.

945. **Love is blind/But the neighbors ain't,/So don't make love/At the garden gate.**
—Courtesy of Mary Ferrario O'Brien.

946. **Man asks young woman for a dance. She accepts. They start dancing. He: I bet you're married, aren't you?/She: Not any more. He: That means you're divorced?/She: Very good! He: So, you are a smart ass, too?/She: Better than a dumb ass!**
—Lisa Brasil, on her first encounter with future husband, Joe Brasil.

947. **Ms. Clark, the 80-year-old with the bad hip, said she did not suffer from the solitude either. Her chair is positioned to look through the big picture window that dominates her living room.//On a clear day, you can see across her land and all the way, 60 miles or so, to Laramie Peak. It is a landscape drenched with the memory, she said, of her husband, Leo, who died last year after a long illness, and the six daughters they raised together on the land.//"I sit, and I look," she said.**
—Kirk Johnson, The New York Times, 12/10/2009, p. A1.

948. **Nobody loves me. It's tragic.**
—analysand to her analyst (1/31/2010).

949. **Man will only become better when you make him see what he is like.**
—*Anton (Pavlovich) Chekhov, 1860-1904, Russian play-wright and short-story writer.*

950. **Man's capacity for justice makes democracy possible; but man's inclination to injustice makes democracy necessary.**
—*Reinhold Niebuhr, theologian.*

951. **My father was a perfect example of how far being an ornery old bastard can take you.**
—*MaLou Manges, daughter of the legendary Texas oilman and rancher, Clinton Manges, 87, in an obituary in "The San Antonio Express News," as reported by Douglas Martin in Obituaries, <u>The New York Times</u>, September 29, 2010, p. B11.*

952. **My question to them is: When is the right time? If not now, when? If not us, who?**
—*President Barack Obama, on those seeking to delay a health care overhaul (*The New York Times, *3/9/2010, p. A1).*

953. **Martinis are like breasts. One isn't enough and three is too many.**
—*Herb Caen, famed San Francisco columnist.*

954. **Master of the bright thunderbolt, save men from painful ignorance.**
—*The stoic poet Cleanthes' hymn to Zeus.*

955. **May you be in heaven before the devil knows you're dead.**
—*old Irish saying.*

956. **One learns from defeat, not from victory.**
—*Related by Bobby Jones, golf immortal.*

957. **Momma's kids, Poppa's maybe.**
—*Italian folk wisdom, courtesy of Mary Ferrario O'Brien.*

958. **Not everybody trusts a painting, but people believe photographs.**
—*Ansel Adams (1902-1984) U.S. photographer.*

959. **Never, never, never believe any war will be smooth and easy or that anyone who embarks on the strange voyage can measure the tides and hurricanes he will encounter. The statesman who yields to war fever must realize that once the signal is given, he is no longer the master of policy but the slave of unforeseeable and uncontrollable events.**
—*Sir Winston Churchill*

960. **My name is Lyndon Baines Johnson. I'm your goddamn president and I'm here to tell you my office and the people of the United States are behind you.**
—*President Johnson, shining a flashlight on his face while speaking to the people gathered in a darkened refugee shelter in New Orleans, after Hurricane Betsy in 1965.*

961. **Ms. Grandin [Temple] was born in 1947 in Boston, and her autism was diagnosed when she was a child. At that time most psychiatrists considered it a mental disorder caused by cold, withholding "refrigerator" mothers.**
—*Alessandra Stanley, "Television Review," The New York Times, February 5, 2010.*

962. **My darling, I've ached for you every single day. How I wish you were here to help as I've barely made a dent in throwing out your stuff.//All my love...**
—*In Memoriam column, The New York Times, May 4, 2009.*

963. **MOMENT OF LOVE**

She touches his face,
wiping away — what,
a piece of dirt?
Or just an excuse for
closing the distance between them.
His response: a tug at her waist,
his fingers pulling her tighter in.
He brushes a hair off her face,
a reciprocal gesture?
A moment's affection,
a declaration of love
on the DeKalb Avenue station,
both waiting to board

the train for the city.
The subway rumbles in,
couple jostled,
the tender moment,
ephemeral,
lost in the roar
of the Q.
—Mel Glenn, "Metropolitan Diary," The New York Times, July 12, 2010, p. A18.

964. **Never spit in the face of love.**
—Sarah Matthews, as told to her by her grandfather (The New York Times, Weddings/Celebrations, 4/4/2010, p. 13).

965. **I slept with my French husband halfway through our first date.**
—the opening sentence of Elizabeth Baird's Lunch in Paris: A Love Story, With Recipes.

966. **Nature dangles sex to keep us walking towards the cliff.**
—Piet, in John Updike's The Couples.

967. **Pluck the chicken, but don't make it scream.**
—Emperor Jacques I (Jean-Jacques Dessalines), ruler of Haiti, 1804-06, referring to taxation of the populace.

968. **Nature robbed the flesh that she might the more lavishly adorn the mind and heart and soul of the man.**
—a New York Times reporter, 1886, writing about California notable Thomas Starr King, reputedly a physically fragile and strange-looking man.

969. **One must always apologize for talking about painting.**
—Paul Vale'ry (1871-1945), French poet.

970. **Poor Warren. He wasn't a bad egg, Just weak. He loved women and Ohio.**
—Poet John Ashbery, describing President Warren. G. Harding.

971. **No society can surely be flourishing and happy, of which the far greater part of the members are poor and miserable.**
—Adam Smith, 1723-1790, Scottish economist.

972. **Power grows out of the barrel of a gun.**
      —*Mao Zedong*

973. **One fought and battled for hope and grew weary in the struggle... One lived with the pain of the world and with all the cruelty of it... One had to look into hell before one had any right to speak of heaven.**
      —*Bertrand Russell (1872-1970), English philosopher, mathematician and Nobel laureate, told to fellow Non-Conscription activist, Constance Malleson, one evening in 1916.*

974. **Perhaps now that Big Brother [italics] is going off the air, we can have a successor: we put a man and a woman in the same house, and see how long it is before they start braining each other with frying pans. It will be called Marriage [italics].**
      —*Nicholas Lezard, "Down and Out in London," New Statesman, 9/7/2009.*

975. **The Germans and the French are little trouble, but the Americans have an unquenchable thirst for knowledge, though they do not seem to mind if the information they are given is, to say the least, casual.**
      —*How to Avoid People (1963), B. A. Young, in the Schmulowitz Collection of Wit & Humor, San Francisco Public Library.*

976. **No woman has ever loved a man for his good character. She may respect him, admire him, be fond of him, but he is never the man for whom she will toss her bonnet over the windmills of the world.**
      —*Helen Brown Norden – The Hussy's Handbook (1942) - in the Schmulowitz Collection of Wit & Humor, San Francisco Public Library.*

977. **People who complete their education do not recidivate.**
      —*Vid Beldavs, a spokesperson for prison reform, commenting on the vital importance of inmate educational programs.*

978. **The first counterfeit bill he passed on his fellow citizens, in 1938, was a very bad copy of a one dollar bill.**
      When his career as a counterfeiter came to an end, in 1948, he was still turning out the same crude dollar bills from the same kind of inferior plates, on the same hand-driven printing press in the same corner of the same kitchen of the same top-

floor tenement flat, and he never turned out more counterfeit dollars than he needed to support his dog and himself.
—*"Mister 880," by St. Clair McKelway, 1949, "tells the story of an elderly counterfeiter who not only was no artist but in fact provoked a manhunt 'that exceeded in intensity and scope any other manhunt in the chronicles of counterfeiting' precisely because his ineptitude was so bewildering" (Essay/Craig Seligman, <u>The New York Times Book Review</u>, 3/7/2010, p. 23).*

979. **One of the amusements of idleness is reading without the fatigue of close attention; and the world therefore swarms with writers whose wish is not to be studied, but to be read.**
—*Dr. Samuel Johnson, English lexicographer and writer, 1709-1784.*

980. **Old age is like being on death row, but with more privileges.**
—*JMM*

981. **Schizophrenics have unresolved gayness.**
—*A personal communication.*

982. **Never before in our history have these forces been so united against one candidate as they stand today. They are unanimous in their hatred for me - and I welcome their hatred.**
—*Franklin Delano Roosevelt, in a radio address to the nation prior to the 1936 election.*

983. **No, It wasn't worth one.**
—*Harry Patch, 111, Britain's last World War I Army veteran, when asked shortly before his death if the efforts invested by the Allied Powers in World War I was worth the lives that were lost in it (<u>The New York Times</u>, July 26, 2009, p. 20).*

984. **Question: "What do you think of him?" Answer: "He doesn't make me think."**
—*Christopher Hitchens, when asked his opinion of British Prime Minister David Cameron.*

985. **Teens go through phases; this is not an oddity. Monday we like blue, Tuesday we like orange, Wednesday we like girls and Thursday we like boys. Do not be fooled. Sexuality is not something we can assume. While teenagers are still growing,**

their minds are influenced by a variety of factors, including pop culture, friends, even absolute strangers.
—Cree Bautista, in his essay in the Common Application for admittance to the freshman class at New York University. (The New York Times, August 11, 2010, p. A9).

986. **She may befuddle others, but for her, life is joyful. She takes obvious pleasure in being an eccentric in a tradition with no shortage of odd heroes and saints.**

   "You can really be quite strange, and the Catholic church will canonize you eventually," she says. She loves eating the flesh and blood of Christ in the Eucharist, which she believes is a carnivorous meal, not a metaphor. She loves gay synth-pop bands.
   —Mark Oppenheimer, describing the lesbian writer and blogger, Eve Tushnet, in "Beliefs", The New York Times, June 5, 2010, p. A14.

987. **Science is not only a disciple of reason, but, also, one of romance and passion.**
   —Stephen Hawking, 68, theoretical physicist, writer, and co-author of The Grand Design, his latest book.

988. **One foot in the grave, the other sliding.**
   —Verna Bairn, 67, speaking about her hometown, Oshkosh, Nebraska, The New York Times, 12/10/2009.

989. **Religion is the tragedy of mankind.**
   —A. N. Wilson, British author, before his reversion to the Church of England.

990. **San Francisco is a mad city inhabited for the most part by perfectly insane people whose women are of remarkable beauty.**
   —Rudyard Kipling, 1889, in an account discovered by San Franciscan John Dobby – (Leah Garchik column, San Francisco Chronicle, August, 2009).

991. **Private Affluence, Public Squalor.**
   —SNN

992. **She was 17. She just wanted to live, that's all. She loved to live.**
—*Antonio Olivo, distraught father of Sofia, burned to death in an arson-set apartment fire, <u>The New York Times</u>, 12/29/2009, p. A22).*

993. **The Devil under form of Baboon is our grandfather.**
—*Charles Darwin*

994. **STYLE CREDO My style is completely schizophrenic. I can be feminine, sexy, over the top, masculine, androgynous. I see fashion as a way to play with your personality, to flirt with a part of yourself. It's like when you go on a date with someone. You're excited, you dress up, and you look phenomenal. When you get dressed, you should always be dating someone — even if it's just yourself.**
—*Anna Dello Russo, fashion director at large for Vogue Japan, (PULSE, Karin Nelson, <u>The New York Times</u>, Sunday, September 19, 2010).*

995. **The "empty room in the heart that is the essence of addiction."**
—*Gail Caldwell, former alcoholic, author of <u>Let's Take the Long Way Home/A Memoir of Friendship</u>.*

996. **So we beat on, boats against the current, borne back ceaselessly into the past.**
—*The final sentence in F. Scott Fitzgeralds's <u>The Great Gatsby.</u>*

997. **She was always bossy and now she is bossy in hell.**
—*Public Eavesdropping, (Leah Garchik, <u>San Francisco Chronicle</u>, 2/24/2009).*

998. **SILENCE, SILENCE: in a thousand senses I proclaim the indispensable worth of Silence, our only safe dwelling-place often.**
—*Thomas Carlyle, 1795-1881, Scottish essayist and historian, in a letter to a friend in 1840.*

999. **Silent gratitude isn't very much to anyone.**
—*Gertrude Stein, 1874-1946, American writer in France.*

1000. ***Simplicity* is the ultimate sophistication.**
—*Leonardo da Vinci, 1452-1519, Italian artist, architect, and engineer.*

1001. **So shalt thou feed on death,**
that feeds on men
And death once
dead, there's no more dying then.
—*William Shakespeare, Sonnet 146.*

1002. **So tall!**
—*Russian ballerina Anna Pavlova's first impression of New York City.*

1003. **So the end result of the long campaign against government is**
that we've taken a disastrously wrong turn. America is now on
the unlit, unpaved road to nowhere.
—*Paul Krugman, <u>The New York Times</u>, August 9, 2010, p. A19.*

1004. **Tell my mother I died for my country. I thought I did it for the**
best. Useless, useless...
—*John Wilkes Booth, as he lay dying from a gunshot wound to the neck*
after refusing to surrender to authorities following his assassination of
President Abraham Lincoln on April 14, 1864.

1005. **The first child you bathe, the second you dust.**
—*Old Chinese saying.*

1006. **Sweeter wrath is by far than the honeycomb dripping with**
sweetener...
—*Homer, 9th-century B.C. Greek epic poet: reputed author of the <u>Iliad</u>*
and <u>Odyssey.</u>

1007. **Takes one to catch one.**
—*Franklin Delano Roosevelt, when asked in 1934 why he had chosen a*
"crook."

1008. **The jury rejected his plea of not guilty by reason of insanity and**
sentenced him to loaf in prison.
—*JMM*

1009. **Suicide is a path out of pain, an extreme act by a disordered,**
hopeless spirit and psyche that sees no alternative. To suffer so

greatly deserves the empathy of all and, in military cases, that of our commander in chief.
—*Kristine A. Munholland, bereavement coordinator for Kaiser Permanente Hospice and adjunct assistant professor of social work at Portland [OR] State University (<u>The New York Times</u>, 12/20/2009).*

1010. **The fact that slaughter is a horrifying spectacle must make us take war more seriously, but not provide an excuse for gradually blunting our swords in the name of humanity. Sooner or later someone will come along with a sharp sword and hack off our arms.**
—<u>On War</u>, *by Carl von Clausewitz (1780-1831).*

1011. **The fiery force is nothing more than the life force as we know it. It is the flame of desire and love, of sex and beauty, of pleasure and joy as we consume and are consumed, as we burn with pleasure and burn out in time.**
—<u>In the Hub of the Fiery Force, Collected Poems</u>, *1934-2003, Harold Norse [1917-2009].*

1012. **The difference between sex for money and sex for free, is that sex for money always costs a lot less.**
—*Sebastian Horsley, "England's low-rent Oscar Wilde" – <u>The New York Times</u>, Sunday, August 23, 2009.*

1013. **The primatologist Frans de Waal tells a story about a bonobo. One day, a starling smashed into the glass of the ape's enclosure and fell to the ground. The bonobo approached the stunned bird and set it on its feet; the bird failed to move. So the ape carried it to the top of a tall tree, unfolded its wings and set it free like a paper aeroplane. But the starling spiralled back to the ground. The bonobo descended the tree and protected the bird for some time. Eventually, the bird recovered and flew to safety.**
—*Mark Vernon, "More than a feeling," <u>New Statesman</u>, London, 6 September, 2010, p. 38.*

1014. **The frankest and freest product of the human mind and heart is a love letter. The writer gets his limitless freedom of statement and expression from his sense that no stranger is going to see what he is writing.**
—*Mark Twain (pen name of Samuel Langhorne Clemens).*

1015. **There is a great deal of symbolism of this kind of life, but as a rule we pass it by without heeding it.//When I set myself the task of bringing to light what human beings keep hidden within them, not by the compelling power of hypnosis, but by observing what they say and what they show, I thought the task was a harder one than it really is. He that has eyes to see and ears to hear may convince himself that no mortal can keep a secret. If his lips are silent, he chatters with his fingertips; betrayal oozes out of him at every pore. And thus the task of making conscious the most hidden recesses of the mind is one which it is quite possible to accomplish.**
—Sigmund Freud, Volume VII, The Standard Edition of the Complete Psychological Works of Sigmund Freud, pp. 77-78.

1016. **The Sarah Bernhardt family—now, *there's* a family. The mother made whores of her daughters as soon as they turned thirteen.**
—a conversation overheard in a Paris restaurant by Edmond de Goncourt (1822-1896, French art critic, novelist, and historian), referring to the mother of the famous French actress Sarah Bernhardt (1845-1923).

1017. **The greatest derangement of the mind is to believe in something because one wishes it to be so.**
—Louis Pasteur, 1822-1895, French chemist and bacteriologist.

1018. **The heart that loves is forever young.**
—Greek proverb.

1019. **The poet's, the writer's, duty is to write about these things. It is his privilege to help man endure by lifting his heart, by reminding him of the courage and honor and hope and pride and compassion and pity and sacrifice which have been the glory of his past.**
—U.S author and novelist William Faulkner, in his acceptance speech after being awarded the Nobel Prize in Literature in 1949.

1020. **Truly, he who has seen, heard, understood, and recognized his own self, to him this whole world is known.**
—from the Upanishad, Hindu treatises, usually in dialogue form, composed between the 8th and 6th centuries B.C, and first written A.D. c1300.

1021. This is the baddest white dude I've ever seen in my life.
—Magic Johnson, recalling his first collegiate all-star meeting as a teammate with Larry Bird, preceding their epic professional basketball rivalry - in the HBO documentary "Magic & Bird: A Courtship of Rivals." (Bird's first impression of Johnson was: "Well I thought he was very good, there's no question about it".

1022. The Bible.
—Steve Bercu, owner of BookPeople in Austin, Texas, when asked for the name of the book most frequently stolen from his bookstore (The New York Times Book Review, p. 23, 12/23/2009).

1023. Tell me the truth, oh, shoes,
Where disappeared the feet?
The feet of pumps so shoddy,
With buttondrops like dew —
Where is the little body?
Where is the woman, too?
All children's shoes — but where
Are all the Children's feet?
—Poet Abraham Sutzkever, in A Vogn Shikh (A wagon of Shoes), 1942, describing a wagon filled with a pile of "throbbing shoes", once worn by murdered Jews, rattling through the alleys of Vilna, Lithuania.

1024. We need to worry a lot less about how to communicate our actions and much more about what our actions communicate.
—Admiral Mike Mullen, Chairman of the U.S. Joint Chiefs of Staff, speaking on how best to interact positively with the Muslim world - August, 2009.

1025. The best gift we parents can give our children is for them to see our eyes light up when they enter the room.
—an unnamed elementary school teacher, contributed by Bruce Harville.

1026. The fact of the matter is that there is a little bit of the totalitarian buried somewhere, way down deep, in each and every one of us.
—George F. Kennan, b. 1904, U.S. author and diplomat.

1027. The only bad thing about Cal [University of California, Berkeley] was leaving.
—Gary Freedman, '66.

1028. **When they are about to deliver, Tanzanian mothers often say to their older children, "I'm going to go and fetch the new baby; it is a dangerous journey and I may not return."**
—*Amy Grossman, on the risks of childbirth in less-developed countries – The New York Times, 5/10/2009.*

1029. **The greatest advantage one can well get in war is to do what your enemy does not dream of! Then you have him. CN**
—*General Sir Charles James Napier, 1782-1853, British general, conqueror of Scinde.*

1030. **There was a terrible stench, intermingled with the smell of lime chloride. There were fat and persistent flies – an extraordinary number of them. What were they doing here, among pine trees, on well-trodden ground?**
—*Vasily Grossman, Russian writer and World War II Red Army combat correspondent, imagining what must have been going through the minds of the doomed, newly-arrived men, women and children at the Nazi extermination camp Treblinka, near Warsaw, Poland, where in one year over 875,000 camp inmates had been murdered. (The New York Times Book Review, October 17, 2010, p. 15).*

1031. **The most beautiful things in the world cannot be seen or even touched, they must be felt with the heart.**
—*Helen Keller, 1880-1968, lecturer and author, blind and deaf since infancy.*

1032. **The mass loves strong men.//The mass is female.**
—*Benito Mussolini ("Il Duce"), 1883-1945, Italian Fascist leader: premier of Italy 1922-1943.*

1033. **The most beautiful girl can only give what she has. Such as were rich, gave in addition a part of their money.**
—*a French proverb.*

1034. **The world's best athlete is a girl with four legs.**
—*Joe Drape, The New York Times sports columnist, September 7, 2009, referring to the 3-year-old filly, Rachel Alexandra, following her "heart-pounding" victory in the Woodward Stakes.*

1035. **The worst thing about dying is that it is so unsexy.**
—*JMM*

1036. **There are two things that are important in politics. The first is money, and I can't remember what the second one is.**
—*Marcus "Mark" Hanna (1837-1903), the premier political operative of his era.*

1037. **The only thing that can never be taken from us is the love we give away.**
—*Forrest Church*

1038. **The owl of Minerva spreads its wings only with the falling of the dusk.**
—*Hegel, Georg Wilhelm Friedrich, German philosopher (1770-1831).*

1039. **The people, Sir, are a great beast.**
—*Alexander Hamilton, 1757-1804, first U.S. Secretary of the Treasury 1789-1797.*

1040. **They fuck you up, your mum and dad...**
—*Philip Larkin, British poet.*

1041. **They have learned nothing and forgotten nothing.**
—*Charles-Maurice de Talleyrand, referring to the French Bourbons.*

1042. **Think rich, look poor.**
—*Andy Warhol*

1043. **To me the biggest difference between being in Iraq and back home is that now when I am commuting to and from work I don't have the constant, gnawing fear that suddenly my vehicle will be lifted up in the air by a huge explosion and fireball.**
—*William T. Smith, a former marine staff sergeant and rifle company squad leader, when asked what was the biggest difference between being in Iraq and back home the U.S. [No I.E.D's].*

1044. **Washington, May 25, 1862   1 1/2 P.M./Major General Mc-Clellan//The enemy is moving North in sufficient force to draw Banks before him - precisely in what force we cannot tell - [...] The time is near when you must either attack Richmond or give up the job and come to the defense of Washington - Let me hear from you instantly - A. Lincoln**
—*President Abraham Lincoln, to Union Major General George Brinton McClellan, May 25, 1862.*

1045. **The ultimate measure of a man is not where he stands in moments of comfort, but where he stands at times of challenge..."**
—*Martin Luther King, Jr.*

1046. **The world began without the human race and will certainly end without it.**
—*Claude L'evi-Strauss, 1909-2009, anthropologist, writer and adventurer.*

1047. **There are two ways of spreading light: to be a candle or the mirror that reflects it.**
—*Edith Wharton (1862-1937)*

1048. **Then you leave the office and somebody says: "Hey, dude, you must be nervous. Here's what I do. I picture everyone naked. That gets my mind off it."**
—*Jimmy Fallon, host of NBC's Late Night show.*

1049. **This is our misery and this is our flesh.**
—*A distraught Iraqi man crying out amid the bloody carnage of a devastating suicide bombing attack in Baghdad, in August, 2009.*

1050. **We all have to recognize, no matter how great our strength, that we must deny ourselves the license to do always as we please.**
—*Harry S. Truman, speaking of the United States.*

1051. **They are able to count [sex] at its true value... They recognize the essential impersonality of sex attraction which we may well envy them.**
—*Margaret Mead, 1901-78, U.S. anthropologist, referring to the sexual mores of the Samoan culture.*

1052. **They couldn't hit an elephant at this dist...**
—*Last words of Union General John Sedgwick, shot in the face after failing to take cover and scoffing at the danger posed by Confederate sharpshooters, during the Battle of the Wilderness, Spotsylvania, 1864.*

1053. **They only scream once.**
—*Jean-Claude Singbatile, high school student, describing people bludgeoned to death by Congolese rebels. (Quote of the Day, The New York Times, 3/28/2010).*

1054. **We were told that they [federal troops] wished merely to pass through our country ... to seek gold in the Far West ... Yet before the ashes of the council fire are cold, the Great Father is building his forts among us. You have heard the sound of the white soldier's axe upon the Little Piney. His presence here is ... an insult to the spirits of our ancestors. Are we then to give up their sacred graves to be plowed for corn? Dakotas, I am for war.**
      —*Red Cloud [1822-1909], in a speech at council in Laramie, Wyoming, 1866.*

1055. **This is a mortal wound. Take care of that pistol. It is undischarged and still cocked. It might go off and do harm. I did not intend to fire at him.**
      —*Alexander Hamilton, fatally injured in his duel in 1804 with his political adversary, Aaron Burr.*

1056. **This population is one of the happiest in the world.**
      —*Alexis de Tocqueville, in a letter to his father about the Americans he was meeting in the U.S., 1831-1832.*

1057. **Travel and change of place impart new vigor to the mind.**
      —*Seneca, Lucius Annaeus (c4 B.C. - 65 A.D.), Roman philosopher and playwright.*

1058. **To punish me for my contempt for authority, fate has made me an authority myself.**
      —*Albert Einstein*

1059. **You think too much. Life's not that simple.**
      —*A mother's advice to her son.*

1060. **Wisdom comes only through suffering.**
      —*Aeschylus (525-456 B.C.)*

1061. **To hold happiness is to hold the understanding that the world passes away from us, that the petals fall and the beloved dies. No amount of mockery, no amount of fashionable scowling will keep any of us from knowing and savoring the pleasure of the**

sun on our faces or save us from the adult understanding that it cannot last forever.
—*Amy Bloom, Essay, The New York Times Book Review, 1/31/2010, p. 23.*

1062. **Time, that indifferent destroyer of all things mortal, seems to stay its scythe...**
—*SNN*

1063. **To say that force may sometimes be necessary is not a call to cynicism - it is a recognition of history; the imperfections of man and the limits of reason.**
—*Barack Obama, in his Nobel Peace Prize acceptance address.*

1064. **Travel is fatal to prejudice, bigotry and narrow-mindedness. Broad, wholesome, charitable views of men and things cannot be acquired by vegetating in one little corner of the earth all one's lifetime.**
—*Mark Twain*

1065. **Ultimately Alan's job is to get all of us to play together. Sometimes when you can't hear, you just go with the stick [baton].**
—*Carol Webb, violinist with the New York Philharmonic, speaking of the new music director Alan Gilbert's change of seating arrangements for the musicians, and its effect on the sound of the various instruments. [The New York Times, 9/22/2009].*

1066. **Virtue itself turns vice, being misapplied.**
—*Father Lawrence, in William Shakespeare's play, "Romeo and Juliet".*

1067. **When you say one thing - and mean your mother.**
—*A Freudian slip.*

1068. **Was it permitted to believe that there was nowhere upon the earth or above the earth, a heaven for hogs, where they were requited for all this suffering?**
—*Upton Sinclair, "The Jungle".*

1069. **We must hang together. Else, we shall most assuredly hang separately.**
—*Benjamin Franklin, speaking of the colonies of the United States, in their defiance of the British Crown.*

1070. **We are what we repeatedly do. Excellence, therefore, is not an act, but a habit.**
—*Aristotle, 384-322 B.C., Greek philosopher.*

1071. **We free thinkers who regard Renan as an example do not take shelter behind dogma from the doubts raised by our intellect. The light of reason is our beacon. But neither —unlike the Catholic priest anathematizing dissent from his bully pulpit—do we impose upon others our rule of conduct and way of thinking. All we ask of religion—because we are entitled to do so—is that it keep within its temples, that it limit its instruction to the faithful, and that it refrain from unwarranted interference in the civil and political domain.**
—*French Prime Minister, Emile Combes, in 1903, at the dedication of a statue honoring Ernest Renan, French historian and critic, in his home town of Treguier, France.*

✻

1072. **We are all agreed that your theory is crazy. The question that divides us is whether it is crazy enough to have a chance of being correct.**
—*Dr. Niels Bohr, one of the founders of quantum theory, in a remark to a colleague.*

1073. **We love each other no matter what happens.**
—*a young Afghan couple, prior to their death by stoning at the hands of the Taliban, for having had an affair and then eloping.*

1074. **What more helpful to wisdom than the night?**
—*Cyril of Jerusalem*

1075. **We were laughing and dancing our way to the precipice.**
—*Lucie de la Tour du Pin, speaking of the events leading up the French Revolution of 1789.*

1076. **We were owners of thirst and owners of hunger.**
—*Toma Tsamkxao, a member of the Ju'hoansi tribe of hunter-gatherers who roamed the northern region of the Kalahari desert called Nyae Nyae (Smithsonian Magazine, November, 2009, p. 23).*

1077. **We're busy trying to get homosexuals married, but nobody else wants to get married. I don't understand any of that.**
—*former comedy great Mort Sahl, in an interview in the Marin County, CA, Pacific Sun (4/30 - 5/6, 2010).*

1078. **Well, I may be just a Red Jew son-of-a-bitch to them, but I'm keeping Thomas Jefferson alive.**
—*I.F. "Izzy" Stone, American "radical" journalist and muckraker, during the McCarthy years of the 1950's.*

1079. **We will now discuss in a little more detail the Struggle for Existence.**[4]
—*Charles Darwin, On the Origin of Species, ch. 3.*

1080. **Well, maybe he thinks that the law of self-defense, the way God looks at it, is a little broader than the law books have it. ... Maybe it means killing a man in defense of your business, the way you make your money to take care of your wife and child.**
—*Al Capone, when asked how he felt about someone who commits murder.*

1081. **Well, the heart's a wonder.**
—*Says Pegeen Mike in John Millington Synge's comedy, The Playboy of the Western World.*

1082. **What we want to do, in addition to the horrors of fire, is to bring masonry crashing down on top of the Boche [Germans], to kill the Boche and to terrify the Boche.**
—*Arthur Harris, head of the RAF [Royal Air Force] Bomber Command during World War II, speaking to his Air Staff. (New Statesman, London, 21 December 2009 - 3 January 2010, p. 55).*

1083. **When hearing something unusual, do not preemptively reject it, for that would be folly. Indeed, horrible things may be true, and familiar and praised things may prove to be lies. Truth is truth unto itself, not because people say it is.**
—*Ibn al-Nafis, 13th century Egyptian physician.*

1084. **What a good country or a good squirrel should be doing is stashing away nuts for winter.**
—*William H. Gross, managing director of the Pimco Group (November, 2009).*

1085. **What a curse to be a woman! [Kierkegaard] And yet the very worst curse when one is a woman is, in fact, not to understand that it is one.**
—Simone de Beauvoir, French feminist, and author in 1949 of The Second Sex.

1086. **What am I in the eyes of most people?//A nonentity or an oddity or a disagreeable person — someone who has and will have no position in society, in short a little lower than the lowest.//Very well — assuming that everything is indeed like that, then through my work I'd like to show what there is in the heart of such an oddity, such a nobody.**
—Vincent van Gogh (1853-1890), in a letter to his brother, Theo.

1087. **What a sober man has on his mind, a drunk man has on his tongue.**
—Old Russian proverb.

1088. **When it comes to flattery, lay it on with a trowel.**
—the advice given by Benjamin "Dizzy" Disraeli, British Prime Minister 1868, 1874-1880, on how to talk with Queen Victoria.

1089. **When you start to die, don't.**
—Frank Buckles (1901-2009), one of the last surviving veterans of World War I, when asked how he had been able to live so long.

1090. **With the young girls, you promise them heaven, they'll follow you to hell.**
—Harvey Washington, a convicted pimp, The New York Times, October 7, 2009.

1091. **An egg never has a Y chromosome within it. An ejaculate of sperm is bisexual, offering a more or less equal number of female and male whip-tailed sperm, but eggs are inherently female.**
—Natalie Angier, An Intimate Geography.

1092. **Women alone stir my imagination.**
—Virginia Woolf

1093. **When I was a boy I never thought I should be called upon to fight for my country. But I am no better to die for liberty than**

anyone else. If I lose my life I shall be missed by but few; but if the Union be lost, it will be missed by many.
—*Union soldier, in a letter home on the eve of the Battle of Antietam.*

1094. **When you can put something on that missile bigger than a fucking firecracker, come and see me.**
—*General Curtis LeMay, head of America's Strategic Air Command (SAC) following World War II, responding to General Bernard Schriever, head of the new U.S. nuclear missile program. LeMay had asked Schriever how large a warhead an ICBM could carry, and was told it could carry a megaton - a bomb eighty times more powerful than Little Boy, the weapon that had destroyed Hiroshima. (The New York Review of Books, 2/25/2010, p. 30).*

1095. **When wheat is ripening properly, when the wind is blowing across the field, you can hear the beards of the wheat rubbing together. They sound like the pine needles in a forest. It is a sweet, whispering music that once you hear, you never forget.**
—*Norman Borlaug, 1914-2009, American "Plant Scientist Who Fought Famine", Nobel Peace Prize awardee in 1970 – Obituaries, The New York Times, September 14, 2009.*

1096. **When the blind beetle crawls over the surface of the globe, he doesn't realize that the track he has covered is curved. I was lucky enough to have spotted it.**
—*Albert Einstein*

1097. **Where they have burned books, they will end in burning human beings.**
—*Heinrich Heine, 1821.*

1098. **When the marriage is on the rocks, the rocks are in the bed.**
—*Folklore wisdom*

1099. **You have to be fast only to catch a flea.**
—*Dr. Israel M. Gelfand (1913-2009), world-renowned Russian mathematician and professor of mathematics at Rutgers University [Obituaries, The New York Times, 10/8/2009].*

1100. **As you know, I really don't care for Shakespeare's plays. But yours are even worse.**
—Leo Tolstoy, commenting to his younger friend Anton Chekhov about the latter's own plays.

1101. **When you become old...When you become old, you find yourself auditioning for the role of a lifetime; then, after interminable rehearsals, you're finally starring in a horror film – a talentless, irresponsible, and above all low-budget horror film, in which (as is the way with horror films) they're saving the worst for last.**
—Martin Amis, The Pregnant Widow, Knopf, 370 pp., $26.95.

1102. **With all things, and in all things, we are relatives.**
—Sioux

1103. **You can fool all of the people some of the time and some of the people all of the time, but you cannot fool all of the people all of the time.**
—Abraham Lincoln

❈

1104. **You're not too smart, are you? I like that in a man.**
—Actress Kathleen Turner's line from the movie, "Body Heat".

1105. **Ruthless waste makes woeful want.**
—Old maxim

1106. **Yet is it love in the sense that love for a real woman would be love? The ancient Greeks would have had a fine time. Eros? Philia? Storge? Agape? Or is it simply self-delusion, like all love is self-delusion, an evolutionarily advantageous affective disorder, designed to stimulate bonding and repeated sex, and consequently good for the species?**
—Michael Bywater, in his review of "Love and Sex With Robots: the Evolution of Human-Robot Relationships," by David Levy, in the New Statesman, London, 5/5/2008, p. 52.

1107. **Young man, I kill thousands of people every night.**
—*Arthur Harris, head of the RAF Bomber Command in World War II, replying to a police constable who had stopped his speeding car at night as he was being driven to London from Bomber Command headquarters in High Wycombe, and who had admonished him that "You could have killed someone." (New Statesman, London, 21 December 2009 - 3 January 2010, p. 57).*

1108. **You've made it twice, right?**
—*Eleven-year-old boy, who has a seven-year-old sister, quizzing his mother, Christie Gentry, about her relations with his dad his fingers pulling her tighter in. He brushes a hair off her face, a reciprocal gesture? A moment's affection, a declaration of love on the DeKalb Avenue station, both waiting to board the train for the city. The subway rumbles in, couple jostled, the tender moment, ephemeral, lost in the roar of the Q. Mel Glenn, "Metropolitan Diary," The New York Times, July 12, 2010, p. A18.*

1109. **You know you are getting old when you get excited about receiving your first handicapped parking placard from the Dept. of Motor Vehicles.**
—*JMM*

1110. **[one of the] two completely evil men I have ever met.**
—*Felix Frankfurter, 1882-1965, speaking of one of his colleagues on the U.S Supreme Court, associate justice William O. Douglas, 1898-1980.*

1111. **In his good introduction to this volume, editor Taylor reveals Bellow's response to the idea of writing an autobiography—he had "nothing to tell" except that he'd been unbearably busy since getting circumcised.**
—*Bart Schneider, describing Nobel Laureate Saul Bellow's reaction when editor Benjamin Davis suggested to him that he compose his autobiography ("Books", San Francisco Chronicle and SFGate.com, Sunday, November 14, 2010, p. F3).*

1112. **You just go from one apartment to another.**
—*Alberto Arroyo, 94, former jogger, considered to be "the Mayor of Central Park," speaking of his lack of fear of death, in a New York Times interview in 2005 (The Alberto Arroyo obituary, The New York Times, 3/27/2010, by Douglas Martin).*

1113. **You should know that our leaders are big belly people, and they care about themselves more than anyone else. Osman Shenwari, a village mayor in Afghanistan.**
—(Quotation Of The Day, *The New York Times*, 9/18/2010, p. A2).

1114. **The law locks up the hapless felon/
Who steals the goose from off the common,/
But lets the greater felon loose/
Who steals the common from the goose.**
—Anonymous, England, 1821.

1115. **Yesterday is history... Tomorrow is mystery... Today is a gift.**
—(Anna) Eleanor Roosevelt, 1884-1962, U.S. diplomat and author (wife of Franklin Delano Roosevelt).

1116. **Yeah, I used to get depressed watching the news, too. Then I discovered the miracle of apathy.**
—Non Sequitur, Wiley Miller.

1117. **You don't have to be a weatherman to know which way the wind is blowing.**
—Originator unknown

1118. **You will see that "accuracy, accuracy, accuracy," is the first and most urgent, the most constant demand I have made on them.**
—Joseph Pulitzer, 1847-1911, U.S. publisher and journalist, referring to the requirements he placed upon his reporters and editors.

1119. **I feel happy because I'm unique.**
—Edward "Nino" Hernandez, 24, a Colombian, considered the shortest man in the world (2010) at 27 inches (69 cm) tall.

1120. **You may drive out nature with a pitchfork, but she will always return.**
—A Latin proverb.

1121. **You show me a happy homosexual, and I'll show you a gay corpse.**
—Mart Crowley, in *The Boys in the Band*, his 1968 comedic drama about gay men at play - now back in a new Off-Broadway production (March, 2010). [The above quotation is considered to be the most "notorious" line in the play].

1122. **You wine sack, with a dog's eyes, with a deer's heart.**
—*Achilles' bitter comment about Agamemnon, in Richmond Lattimore's 1951 translation of Homer's Iliad.*

1123. **Woe is me.**
—*Albert Einstein, upon learning of the atomic bombing of Hiroshima in 1945.*

1124. **Lincoln had two characteristics: one of purity, and the other, as it were, an insane love [of] telling dirty and smutty stories.**
—*Henry Dummer, one of Abraham Lincoln's lawyer friends, in The Intimate World of Abraham Lincoln, by C. A. Tripp, Thunder's Mouth Press, New York, 2005, p. 36.*

1125. **You make a living by what you get. You make a life by what you give.**
—*Sir Winston Churchill*

1126. **You sons of bitches, give my love to mother!**
—*Francis "Two-Gun" Crowley, while strapped in Sing Sing's electric chair in 1931.*

1127. **Youth is easily deceived because it is quick to hope.**
—*Aristotle, 384-322 B.C., Greek Philosopher: pupil of Plato; tutor of Alexander the Great.*

1128. **Even so, Lincoln's good humor did not erase a persistent moroseness. He was still, as Herndon [Lincoln's law partner] said, "a sad-looking man; his melancholy dripped from him as he walked. His apparent gloom impressed his friends, and created sympathy for him—one means of his great success."[31] In fact, nearly every close friend of the adult Lincoln was well aware of his melancholia. Lincoln himself referred to his gloomy spells as his "hypo" (short for hypochondria, one definition of which in Victorian times was extreme melancholy—depression). It is true that Lincoln told folksy anecdotes to illustrate his points," wrote Stephen B. Oates in "Abraham Lincoln: The Man Behind the Myths." "But humor was also tremendous therapy for this depression—it was a device to 'whistle down sadness,' as Judge Davis put it." Lincoln agreed, saying of himself: "I laugh because I must not weep— that's all, that's all" and "I tell you the truth when I say that a funny story, if it has the element of genuine**

wit, has the same effect on me that I suppose a good square drink of whiskey has on an old toper; it puts new life into me."[12]

—*The Intimate World of Abraham Lincoln, by C. A. Tripp, Thunder's Mouth Press, New York, 2005, pp. 38-9.*

1129. **You lose respect for death. I was just out there putting out the damn fire.**

—*Carl E. Clark, retired USN chief petty officer, explaining his heroism on May 3, 1945, after his ship, the destroyer U.S.S. Aaron Ward, on "picket duty" off Okinawa, was hit by six Japanese kamikaze suicide bombers, spreading death, destruction, and fire throughout the ship. (Mr. Clark is presently, as of December 2010, under consideration to receive the nation's highest military decoration, the Medal of Honor).*

1130. **If slavery is not wrong, nothing is wrong. I cannot remember when I did not so think, and feel.**

—*Abraham Lincoln*

1131. **I find it harder and harder every day to live up to my blue china.**

—*Oscar Wilde, 1854-1900, Irish writer and wit.*

1132. **Paige and I always meet on effusively affectionate terms; and yet he knows perfectly well that if I had his nuts in a steel trap I would shut out all human succor and watch that trap till he died.**

—*The Autobiography of Mark Twain, Volume 1. [Paige was an acquaintance who had convinced Twain to invest a large sum of money on a worthless invention].*

1133. **I can clearly foresee that nothing but the rooting out of slavery can perpetuate the existence of our union, by consolidating it in a common bond of principle.**

—*George Washington, in a prediction to an English visitor in 1798.*

1134. **She sells seashells by the seashore.**

—*Mary Anning, the impoverished and uneducated girl who inspired this "tongue-twister".*

1135. **What we need is a way to reach Joe Bagadoughnuts in Wherever, Louisiana, because that's where these cases are turning up.**
—*John S. Odom, Jr.*

1136. **Nine scorpions in a bottle.**
—*Oliver Wendell Holmes, Jr. (the Great Dissenter), 1841-1935, supposedly describing himself and his eight fellow U.S. Supreme Court justices.*

1137. **Bad times. We wake up with a painful auguring, and after exploring a little to know the cause find it is the odious news in each day's paper, the infamy that has fallen on Massachusetts, that clouds the daylight, & takes away the comfort of every hour. We shall never feel well again until that detestable law [the Fugitive Slave Act of 1850] is nullified in Massachusetts & until the government is assured that once and for all it cannot and shall not be executed here. All I have, and all I can do shall be given & done in opposition to the execution of the law.**
—*Ralph Waldo Emerson, 1803-1882, U.S. essayist and poet.*

1138. **[He had] nothing to tell except that he'd been unbearably busy ever since getting circumcised.**
—*Novelist and Nobel Prize winner Saul Bellow's response to the idea of writing his autobiography*

1139. **Saints should always be judged guilty until they are proved innocent.**
—*George (Eric Arthur Blair) Orwell, 1903-1950, English novelist and essayist.*

1140. **We may please ourselves with the prospect of free and popular governments. But there is great danger that those governments will not make us happy. God grant they may. But I fear that in every assembly, members will obtain an influence by noise not sense. By meanness, not greatness. By ignorance, not learning. By contracted hearts, not large souls...**
—*John Adams, from a letter dated April 22, 1776, while serving in the First Continental Congress. (Courtesy of Francesca Mihok, Burlington, Vt., Nov. 4, 2010, in Letters to the Editor, The New York Times, November 5, 2010).*

1141. **Every night frenzied young girls invade my bed. Last night I had three of them to keep me company. I'm going to stop leading this wild life and install a more responsible woman in the house and work like mad.**
—Paul Gaugin, from Tahiti, in Gaugin by Himself, edited by Belinda Thomson.

1142. **At the beginning of the war, 1861, he has black hair, and six months later he looks like an entirely changed person, with the white beard, white hair. His family can't believe it.**

   They look at pictures of him they see published, and they don't think it's the same person.
—Elizabeth Brown Pryor, speaking of Confederate General Robert E. Lee, on the PBS series, "American Experience".

1143. **These Libraries have improv'd the general Conversation of the Americans, made the common Tradesmen & Farmers as intelligent as most Gentlemen from other countries, and perhaps have contributed to some degree to the Stand so generally made throughout the Colonies in Defence of their Privileges.**
—Benjamin Franklin, commenting later in his autobiography on his founding in 1731 of the Library Company of Philadelphia, America's first successful lending library.

1144. **Old Guard Republicans of the blackest and most violently Neanderthal stripe.**
—Cooking maven Julia Childs, writing about her family's political leanings.

1145. **My old father used to have a saying that "If you make a bad bargain, hug it all the tighter."**
—Abraham Lincoln, Letter No. 6, dated February 25, 1842, to his friend Joshua Speed, (ibid, p. 264).

1146. **This country has come to feel the same when Congress is in session as we do when the baby gets hold of a hammer. It's just a question of how much damage he can do before you take it away from him.**
—Will Rogers, American humorist, The New York Times, July 5, 1930.

1147. **My Mother, My Father**

> **My mother—the greatest—and**
> **the prettiest**
> **My father—just handsome—**
> **but the wittiest...**
> **I was raised in the palm of the**
> **hand**
> **By the very best people in this**
> **land**
> **From sun to sun**
> **Their hearts beat as one**
> **My mother—my father—and**
> **love**
> —*Duke Ellington, written for his 1963 musical show, "My People"* .

1148. **Patriotism is the last refuge of a scoundrel.**
   —*From "BOSWELL, Life of Johnson," April 7, 1775; Bartlett's Familiar Quotations, 17th edition, 327:25.*

1149. **Four things belong to a judge: to hear courteously, to answer wisely, to consider soberly, and to decide impartially.**
   —*Socrates, 469?-399 B.C., Athenian philosopher.*

1150. **When the facts change then my opinion changes; and you, sir?**
   —*John Maynard Keynes, 1st Baron, 1883-1946, English economist and writer.*

1151. **Great scientists attempt to generalize their theories to cover an unsuspected breadth of phenomena.**
   —*Richard Lewontin, an observation.*

1152. **The "missing five ounces."**
   —*What English Victorians (1870-1875) referred to as the lesser dimensions of the female brain compared to the male brain.*

1153. **Tenzing and I had spent a good part of the previous night quaffing copious quantities of hot lemon drink and, as a consequence, we arrived on top with full bladders.**

Having just paid our respects to the highest mountain in the world, I had no choice but to urinate on it.
—*Sir Edmund Hillary (1919-2008) on scaling Mount Everest in 1953, from "View From the Summit" (1999). [Contributed by Larry Habegger, "The Quotable Traveler," San Francisco Chronicle, Feb. 27, 2011.].*

1154. **...where so many people are lost in thought because it's such unfamiliar territory.**
—*U.S. Secretary of Defense Robert M. Gates (2011), speaking of the political establishment in the nation's capital.*

1155. **The assumption that animals are without rights and the illusion that our treatment of them has no moral significance is a positively outrageous example of Western crudity and barbarity.**
   Universal compassion is the only guarantee to morality.
—*Arthur Schopenhauer, 1788-1860, German philosopher.*

1156. **...was apt to smile into your face with a subtle but amiable perception, and yet with a sort of remote absence; you were all there for him, but he was not all there for you.**
—*William Dean Howells, 1837-1920, U.S. author and critic, commenting on his friend Mark Twain, 1835-1910, U.S. author and humorist, in his memoir "My Mark Twain" (1910).*

1157. **No nation, howsoever mighty, occupies a foot of land that was not stolen.**
—*Mark Twain [Samuel Langhorne Clemens], 1835-1910, U.S. author and humorist.*

1158. **...[when] pricks were stiff and cunts not loath to take ye stiffness out of them.**
—*Mark Twain, in his privately circulated "faux-Elizabethan" narrative about a certain golden age.*

1159. **[334] These gift calamities.**
—*a father referring to the births of his son and daughter, who were not "consciously" planned – the daughter later suiciding at the age of 22 by jumping out of a window.*

1160. **"As Deputy Chief John A. Adams explained, unlike the South Tower which toppled over, 'ours peeled away like a banana. And we were the banana. We were at the bottom.'"**
—The New York Times, Al Baker, January 17, 2011, in his story about fireman John A. Adams, then a Captain, who, along with five other firemen and a woman named Josephine Harris, whom they were rescuing, survived the catastrophic collapse of the North Tower of the World Trade Center on September 11, 2001, huddled together in the shelter of a stairwell near the ground floor. Ms. Harris, recently deceased (January, 2011), had urged them to go on without her.

1161. **Because I could not stop for**
Death—
He kindly stopped for me—
The carriage held but just
Ourselves—
And Immortality.
—Emily (Elizabeth) Dickinson, 1830-1886, U.S. poet.

1162. **The Naked truth behind Marin teens' coitus email-ruptus [p. 13]**
—The front-page headline story in the "Pacific Sun," (a Marin County, CA, weekly newspaper, Jan. 28 - Feb. 3, 2011), about local teenagers sext-messaging each other, with pictures, on their cell phones.

❋

1163. **This is as it should be, for criminal behavior is essentially an illness, caused largely by sexual maladjustments.**
—Clinton Duffy, former renowned American prison warden and criminal justice reformist.

1164. **I couldn't run backward. I had to run forward. That's the job of a soldier.**
—Army private Barney F. Hajiro, speaking of his actions on October 29, 1945, for which he was awarded the Medal of Honor 56 years later by President Bill Clinton. He had previously been awarded three Distinguished Service Crosses. (The New York Times, Obituaries, Thursday, February 3, 2011, p. A23.) .

1165. **Quod dubitas ne feceris. (When in doubt, Don't.)**
—Pliny "the Elder", A.D. 23-79, Roman naturalist and writer.

1166. **We have walked together in the shadow of a rainbow.**
—*A Native American saying describing a "magical" interaction between man and animal.*

1167. **I've been a racist since 1921. I don't know how they can think that I'm imitating Hitler.**
—*from the diaries of a mistress to Benito Mussolini, describing the fascist dictator's offended feelings in 1938, about the Hitler comparison.*

1168. **We try every way we can do to kill the game, but for some reason, nothing nobody does never hurts it.**
—*Sparky Anderson, famed baseball manager, the first to win the World Series in both leagues, but lose the title as baseball's best "grammarian".*

1169. **A sacred union between a man and a pregnant woman.**
—*American humorist Craig Kilborn's definition of a marriage.*

1170. **Owners still believe that anything with a leg on each corner has a chance to win in Louisville.**
—*Famed sports-writer Red Smith, commenting on the hopes of every racehorse owner that his or her promising 3-year-old has a chance of winning the fabled Kentucky Derby.*

1171. **What I cannot create,**
   I do not understand.
—*once written on a blackboard at the California Institute of Technology, by famed physicist Richard Feynman.*

1172. **They f-ck you up, your mum and dad, they may not mean to, but they do – they fill you with the faults they had, and add some extra, just for you.**
—*poet Philip Larkin, "This Be the Verse".*

1173. **It is advisable to look from the tide pool to the stars and then back to the tide pool again.**
—*John (Ernst) Steinbeck, 1902-1968, U.S. novelist: Nobel prize 1962.*

1174. **For O'Connor, who grew up not far from the house Synge [Irish playwright John Millington Synge] shared with his parsimonious mother– where Synge was, in O'Connor's account, 'slowly roasted on the flames of her widowhood' – the impossible love of Synge and Allgood [Molly - the Irish dramatist] matches the**

divisions that have bedeviled the union of Ireland for generations.
—*Professor Christopher Benfey, in his review of Joseph O'Connor's "Ghost Light"* (*The New York Times Book Review, February 6, 2011, p. 11*).

1175. **From all that he loves, man must part.**
—*an "inescapable Buddhist truth".*

1176. **It is dangerous to show man too often how much he resembles the beasts, without showing him his grandeur. And it is even more dangerous to show him too often his grandeur without also his baseness. It is more dangerous still to let him ignore both.**
—*Blaise Pascal, 1623-1662, French philosopher and mathematician.*

1177. **There was also a day in February [2010] when I had an epiphany. I had lived my life without regrets. I had loved with my whole heart, lived each day for all it was, done my best while doing the right thing, and I was at peace. I realized that by living without fear, I wasn't afraid of what the future may or may not hold. If my time was up, then I could leave this earth satisfied. If I was to live another day, then I would continue according to plan.**
—*Serena Burla, elite long distance runner and all-American 10,000-meter runner in 2006 at the University of Missouri, on being diagnosed in January, 2010, with having a highly malignant tumor in her right leg. (She has now recovered from the surgery to remove the tumor and is running again.)* The New York Times, *March 19, 2011, p. B13.*

1178. **I don't know, honey. It sure beats the hell out of me.**
—*Elizabeth Taylor, U.S. film actress, 1932-2011, when asked once why she had married and divorced so many times (7).*

1179. **Speak with a wise man, there'll be**
   Much to learn; speak with a fool,
All you get is prattle.
Strike a half-empty pot, and it'll make
A loud sound; strike one that is full,
Says Kabir, and hear the silence.
—*Kabir (c. 1440-1518), translated from the Hindi by Arvind Krishna Mehrotra.*

1180. **"If it is deemed necessary that I should forfeit my life," and "mingle my blood" with "the blood of millions in this slave country whose rights are disregarded by wicked, cruel and unjust enactments, I say, let it be done."**
—*John Brown, November 2, 1859, in Charles Town, Virginia, when asked by the court if he wished to speak after being sentenced to death by hanging for leading a raid on the federal arsenal at nearby Harper's Ferry.*

1181. **Dare to ask.**
—*a psychotherapist's reply when he was asked by poet and novelist Jill Bialosky, whose sister, Kim, had committed suicide at the age of 21, what a person should do when it is feared that someone you know is contemplating suicide.*

1182. **"We few, we happy few, we band of brothers;**
       For he today that sheds his blood with me
              Shall be my brother..."
—*William Shakespeare, "Henry V".*

1183. **I'll think of it all tomorrow, at Tara. I can stand it then. Tomorrow, I'll think of some way to get him back. After all, tomorrow is another day.**
—*Scarlett, referring to Rhett, in the final paragraph of Margaret Mitchell's epic novel of the Old South, "Gone With the Wind".*

1184. **Yes, I'm a man, but not *fanatically*.**
—*A Brazilian man, when asked if he was a man after being insulted and not responding in kind. (A humorous anecdote appearing in the travel book "Brazil" by the noted American poet Elizabeth Bishop, 1911-79).*

1185. **There are two words. "He cared." People mock me and maked fun of it. But it's the truth.**
—*William Donald Shaefer, 89, former four-term mayor of Baltimore and later two-term governor of Maryland, when asked in 2006 how he would like to be remembered. (The New York Times, Robert D. McFadden, April 19, 2011, Obituary page, B15).*

1186. **A kind of person whose thought bubble changed at a whim.**
—*a description in the New York Times (April 2011) of a recently deceased New York art curator and celebrated man-about-town.*

1187. **She appealed to journalists not to "suck news out of your finger, but analyze the process on the basis of facts and data which were presented in the trial."**
—*Anna Usachev, referring to the politically-charged trial of the former Russian "oil tycoon", Mikhail B. Khodorkovsky, in Moscow, Russia. (The New York Times, April 16, 2011).*

1188. **If something like this had happened on land, there would have been an immediate public outcry and an investigation. But as I learned, there are no skid marks on the ocean.**
—*Amy Ellis Nutt, 55, winner of the 2011 Pulitzer Prize for Feature Writing ("The Star Ledger," Newark, NJ), awarded as the result of her seven-month investigation and 20-page special section in her newspaper "deeply probing" the mystery of the sinking of a fishing vessel off Cape May, New Jersey, with the loss of six men. (From The New York Times account of the 2011 winners of the Pulitzer Prize for general journalistic excellence).*

1189. **We lived the segregated South...There's an emotion when you come here. A tear comes to your eye for all that started here.**
—*Lily Townsend, 77, of Pensacola, Fla., commenting on the newly-renovated Ebenezer Baptist Church in Atlanta, where the Reverend Dr. Martin Luther King, Jr. preached. (The New York Times, "Quotation of the Day," April 21, 2011, p. A2).*

1190. **I hate being a cowboy, but I was born that way. There's a whole class of women who won't sleep with me because of it.**
—*overheard by Abby DeNicasio while standing in line at a Social Security office in San Rafael, CA, "Pacific Sun", May 6-May 12, 2011, p. 7.*

1191. **Democracy is when the indigent, and not the men of property, are the rulers.**
—*Aristotle, 384-322 B.C. – Greek philosopher: pupil of Plato; tutor of Alexander the Great.*

1192. **I see death approaching gradually without any anxiety or regret. I salute you with great affection and regard, for the last time.**
—*David Hume, 1711-76, Scottish philosopher and historian, in a letter to his beloved friend Hippolyte de Saujon, estranged wife of the Comte de Boufflers and celebrated mistress of the Prince de Conti.*

1193. **I'm glad he died before me.**
—a Ground Zero worker tethered to a respirator, when told of Osama bin Laden's death on May 1, 2011, <u>The New York Times</u>, May 2, 2011, p. F1.

1194. **"A self-described multimedia Shaman, Mr. Cohen compared writing to 'pushing a peanut with my nose.' But a postscript to one of his poems marveled at the beauty that could inexplicably blossom: 'Sometimes when I pick up my pen,' he wrote, "it leaks gold all over the tablecloth.'"**
—Douglas Martin, <u>The New York Times</u>, Obituaries, May 2, 2011, writing about filmmaker, photographer and poet Ira Cohen, dead at age 76.

1195. **You could have spit on that tornado when it went down the Interstate.**
—Darlene Mason, front desk clerk at the Comfort Inn in Fairfield, Alabama, <u>The New York Times</u>, Robbie Brown, May 2, 2011, p. A19.

1196. **There's only two ways to go in these operations – zero to hero.**
—Don Shipley, 49, former Seal member, commenting on Seal Team 6's successful mission to kill or capture Osama bin Laden, <u>The New York Times</u>, Elizabeth Bumiller, May 5, 2011, p. 12.

1197. **No, please don't. I don't need to be confused.**
—Jackie Cooper, former child film-star, when asked in 1951 if he wanted to meet with the father who had abandoned him in infancy, <u>The New York Times</u>, Robert T. McFadden, Obituaries, May 5, 2011, p. B13.

1198. **The prime site of my illness was sexual.**
—Australian poet Les Murray, author of "Killing The Black Dog / A Memoir of Depression," – <u>The New York Times</u>, Book Review, Meghan O'Rourke, Sunday, April 3, 2011, p. 16.

1199. **People grew up in church, so a lot of us lived in shame. What did we do? We wandered around lost. We married men, and then couldn't understand why every night we had a headache.**
—Darlene Maffett, who had two children in eight years of marriage before coming out in 2002. (<u>The New York Times</u>/"Quotation of the Day," January 19, 2011, p. A2).

1200. **My mother—the greatest—and
the prettiest
My father—just handsome—**

but the wittiest...
I was raised in the palm of the
hand
By the very best people in this land
From sun to sun
Their hearts beat as one
My mother—my father—and
love
—"My Mother, My Father" (in the song written by Duke Ellington for his 1963 musical show "My People").

1201. **An outsider only hears the growling, and when he sees the bones fly out from beneath, it is obvious who won.**
—Sir Winston Churchill, comparing Russia's power struggles in the Kremlin with bulldogs fighting under a carpet. (The New York Times, Ellen Barry, May 9, 2011, p. A8).

※

1202. **The joke about him was that he was the youngest person ever to turn 40.**
—Peter Orszag, speaking of his father Steven A. Orszag, a brilliant astrophysicist, who died May 1, 2011 at the age of 68. (He had earned his Ph.D. in astrophysics at Princeton University when he was 23.) – The New York Times, Bruce Weber, May 8, 2011, p. 20.

1203. **... a set of surly & savage beings who have power in their hands and murder in their hearts.**
—Jacob Bailey, of Massachusetts, a British loyalist and Harvard classmate of John Adams, commenting on the leaders of the American Revolution. (He later emigrated to Nova Scotia).

1204. **Another damned, thick, square book! Always scribble, scribble, scribble! Eh! Mr. Gibbon?**
—a remark by the Duke of Gloucester to the great English historian, Edward Gibbon.

1205. **An artist is somebody who produces things people don't need to have.**
—the late American pop artist-provocateur, Andy Warhol.

1206. **But he's not a religious fanatic. He doesn't pray, he drinks.**
      —the cabdriver father of a 26-year-old native Algerian man in New York City, charged on May 12, 2011, with plotting acts of terrorism. (The New York Times, 5/13/2011, p. A21-22).

1207. **If you can't come before then, don't bother coming.**
      —a Marine commander replying to a message that he and his men would be evacuated after dark from a Japanese-held island they had attacked the night before, and who were now surrounded by the enemy and in dire straits. (Smithsonian Magazine, November 2011, p. 34).

1208. **It's about the worst thing you can be in black culture. You're taught to be a man; you have to be masculine. In the black community they think you can pray the gay away.**
      —Don Lemon, gay CNN prime-time weekend anchor. (The New York Times, Bill Carter, May 16, 2001, p. A8.).

1209. **What I still do mourn is the terrible waste of energy the Dog has exacted from me, over my lifetime and especially in my twenty horror years, and how much more I might have achieved if I'd owned a single, healthy mind working on my side.**
      —Les Murray, award-winning Australian poet, in "Killing The Black Dog/A Memoir of Depression," Farrar, Straus and Giroux, New York, 2009, p. 37.

1210. **"I am Mahler," Bernstein [Leonard] said on more than one occasion, implying not so much an actual reincarnation as a repository of his all-embracing musical spirit. Small wonder that Bernstein is buried with a score of Mahler's Fifth Symphony placed over his heart.**
      —Peter G. Davis (Op-Ed, The New York Times, May 18, 2011, p. A17), commenting on former New York Philharmonic conductor Leonard Bernstein's great love and appreciation for the musical works of the noted Viennese composer and conductor, Gustav Mahler.

1211. **Money never sleeps.**
      —Anonymous

1212. **One can make a day of any size and regulate the rising and setting of his own sun and the brightness of its shining.**
      —John Muir, 1838-1914, U.S. naturalist, explorer and writer; born in Scotland. [Courtesy of Roxanne Tancredi.].

1213. **Freedom doesn't need a dialogue.**
—*Louay Hussein, Syrian journalist and activist. (<u>The New York Times,</u> June 3, 2011.).*

1214. **Out here, there is no male gender and no female gender. Our gender is soldier.**
—*Staff Sgt. Vincent Vetterkind, Mehtarlami, Afghanistan, speaking of female soldiers sharing the burdens of war with their male counterparts. (<u>The New York Times</u>, June 21, 2011, p. A4.).*

1215. **Forgive me for everything. Cremate me.**
—*Russian supermodel Anastasia Drozdova, in a suicide note left for her mother in Kiev, Ukraine, in 2009. Earlier in 2008, her good friend and fellow-supermodel Ruslana Korshunova, 20, had suicided in New York City. Both Ruslana and Anastasia had jumped from buildings. (<u>Newsweek</u> magazine, May 9, 2011, p. 52.).*

❊

1216. **Thank you for the free kill. She died in front of me.   Your cheesiness.**
—*Jared Lee Loughner, the paranoid schizophrenic Tucson "shooter," addressing the judge after he had "lowered his head to within inches of the courtroom table and then lifted it and began a loud and angry rant." Loughner had killed six people and wounded 13, the latter including Arizona's U.S. Representative Gabrielle Giffords. [<u>The New York Times</u>/National Briefing (AP), June 15, 2011, p. A16.].*

1217. **Even the jabiru storks seemed to belong to a long-lost age. They'd all stand around in their tatty coachman's livery, stabbing at the frogs and then tossing them back like shots of gin.**
—*John Gimlette, "Travels on South America's Untamed edge," Illus-trated. 358 pp. Alfred A. Knopf. (Liesl Schillinger, in <u>The New York Times Book Review</u>, Sunday, July 24, 2011, p. 17.).*

1218. **When the facts change, I change my opinion.**
   What do you do, Sir?
—*John Maynard Keynes, 1st Baron, 1883-1946, English economist and writer.*

1219. **George Steiner wrote somewhere that an intellectual is someone who can't read a book without a pencil in his or her hand.**
—Geoff Dyer, "The Well-Read Book As a thing of Beauty," (The New York Times Book Review, August 28, 2011, p. 7.).

1220. **He had "gotten old a little bit."**
—Kris Jenkins, 31, to Greg Bishop of The New York Times (April 21, 2011), explaining the probable reason the N.F.L. New York Jets had released him after he had torn his knee ligaments in each of the last two seasons.

1221. **Look, kid, I don't know if one day you'll sing. But remember - always take care of your entrance and your exit. And in the middle, just sing as well as you can.**
—Famed French chanteur Maurice Chevalier, advising aspiring young singer Johnny Hallyday, after Hallyday had sung a few songs for him. (The New York Times, July 16, 2011, p. A 7.).

1222. **If instead of turning our gun scopes toward one another we could turn our telescopes toward the Great beyond, we might be inspired to seek truth instead of destruction.**
—Michael Pravica, associate professor of physics at the University of Nevada, Las Vegas. (To The Editor: July 9, 2011, The New York Times, July 14, 2011, p. A 22.).

❋

1223. **Madness in great ones must not unwatch'd go.**
—the King to Polonius, referring to Prince Hamlet, in Shakespeare's "Hamlet," Act 3, Scene 1.

1224. **Thank you for the free kill. She died in front of me. Your cheesiness.**
—The paranoid schizophrenic Jared Lee Loughner, in a May 25, 2011 angry paranoid rant before a judge. He had been accused of killing six people and wounding 13, including U.S. Representative Gabrielle Giffords, of Arizona. ("National Briefing," The New York Times, June 15, 2011, p. A16.).

1225. **In the wild, male polar bears tend to be loners, who wander long distances through sketchy weather and over shape-shifting ice, with drifting ice pack as home. They go with the floe.**
—*Diane Ackerman, "The Lonely Polar Bear", (<u>The New York Times</u>, July 3, 2011, p. 9.).*

1226. **Never allow yourself to be confused by a handful of killers because good predominates. A bomb makes more noise than a caress, but for each bomb that destroys, there are millions of caresses that nourish life.**
—*Facundo Cabral, 74, Argentinian singer-songwriter, "one of the most eloquent voices of protest against military dictatorships in Latin America, shot to death while on tour in Guatemala." (Larry Rohter, "Singer of Conscience," Obituaries, <u>The New York Times</u>, July 11, 2011, p. B8.).*

1227. **When you're wounded an left on Afghanistan's plains,**
And the women come out to cut up what remains,
Jest roll to your rifle and blow out your brains
An' go to your Gawd like a soldier.
—*"The Young British Soldier" [1892], Rudyard (Joseph) Kipling, 1865-1936, English author and poet, Nobel Prize winner 1907.*

1228. **"Since I've fallen in love with you, I feel like I am 5 years old," she said. "And I feel like I'm 16 years old, and 30 years old and 65 years old, and I feel like I'm 95 years old and we're just holding hands in our rocking chairs."**
—*Trina Willard, 35, in her wedding vows to Joseph Whinney, 44, (San Juan Islands, Wash., Aug. 27, 2011), in VOWS, by Stacey Solie, <u>The New York Times</u>, "Weddings/Celebrations," Sunday, September 11, 2011, p. 16.*

1229. **I was already crushed out on him.**
—*Trina Willard, speaking of her future husband, Joseph Whinney.*

1230. **"Darkness visible" is the long, beautiful essay [William] Styron crafted from his terrible depression, a misama of bottomless despair, that overcame him in 1985 after he gave up drinking. It never really lifted. Even by the standards of suicidal unipolar disorder, Styron's illness reduced him to a near-catatonic state, not merely brushed by Baudelaire's wings of madness but felled by them. He had, like some Miltonic precursor,   been   looking**

through the dark for so long that when it became visible it
nearly blinded him.

*—Andrew O'Hagan, "Styron's Choice", <u>The New York Review of Books</u>,
September 29, 2011, p. 22.*

1231. **The original is not a sentimental celebration of being a kid. It's a
tragic meditation on time. J.M. Barrie draws us into the fantasy
of Neverland, only to make us feel how illusory the "real" world
is, a world of relentless change in which everything slips away
into nothingness.**

*—Tamim Ansary, writer and author, explaining his choice of "Peter
Pan" as the answer to the question "What's your most treasured
book?" ["Books", <u>San Francisco Chronicle</u> and SFGate.com; Sunday,
September 4, 2011, p. F2.].*

1232. **I met Madison and 50 other little rays of hope at the Dorothy
Day Apartments on Riverside Drive in West Harlem. The building
is the sixth in the neighborhood run by Broadway Housing
Communities, and the first to include a day care center serving
both the building and the community.**
**This former drug den is not only beautiful, but it pulses with
pride and hope and happiness.**

*—Charles Blow, <u>The New York Times</u> Op-Ed page, Saturday, September
24, 2011.*

❁

1233. **Reading, study, silence, thought are a bad introduction to
loquacity.**

—William Hazlitt, writer and author.

1234. **I beseech you to treasure up in your hearts these my parting
words. Be ashamed to die until you have won some victory for
humanity.**

*—Horace Mann, Massachusetts-born education reformer and first presi-
dent of Antioch College (Yellow Springs, Ohio), at the 1859 commencement address, just weeks before he died. [Bill Donahue, "Back in the 01'
Hippie Hothouse," <u>The New York Times</u>, Sunday Magazine, September
25, 2011, p. 58.].*

1235. **Mary looked at me like I just sat on her cat.**
—Hope Reeves, describing the look the 83-year-old Block Island, R.I. nurse/philanthropist Mary Donnelly gave her when she asked Mary if she was going to change the name of her Mary D. Fund, when she retired, to the Linda C. fund (Linda Closter, the island's other nurse). [Hope Reeves, "You Are Here," The New York Times, Sunday Magazine, September 18, 2001, p. 34.].

1236. **For to be free is not merely to cast off one's chains, but to live in a way that reflects and enhances the freedom of others.**
—Nelson (Rolihlahla) Mandela, born 1918, president of South Africa, 1994-99: Nobel peace prize 1993.

1237. **Monkey Still Working, Let Baboon Wait Small**
—Displayed on campaign billboards for the re-election of Ellen Johnson Sirleaf, the Harvard-educated, Nobel Prize-winning, 72-year-old president of Liberia. (The opposition billboards proclaim "Too old to hold.") [From article by Adam Nossiter, The New York Times, Monrovia, Liberia, October, 2011.].

1238. **What fresh hell is this?**
—Dorothy (Rothschild) Parker, 1893-1967, U.S. essayist, satirist and critic, employing her standard comment when first answering the telephone. (Joseph H. Berger, The New York Times, 10/1/2011, p. A26.).

1239. **A. The toughest fight I ever had was against John Barleycorn [referring to his struggle against alcoholism].**

B. I was sparring with middleweights to prepare myself for his speed. When the fight finally happened, I never imagined someone could throw punches with such speed. Especially a heavyweight. The punches were coming so fast I thought the referee was sneaking some in too [speaking of his heavyweight fight with Floyd Patterson in 1961, when he was knocked down eight times in four rounds].
—Tom McNeeley, 1937-2011, professional boxer (1958-1966); Bruce Weber, The New York Times, "Obituaries," November 1, 2011, p. A19.

1240. **Both parties deprecated war; but one of them would make war rather than let the nation survive; and the other would accept war rather than let it perish. And the war came.**
—President Abraham Lincoln, in his Second Inaugural address.

1241. **Many kinds of monkeys have a strong taste for tea, coffee and spirituous liquers.**
—*Charles (Robert) Darwin, 1809-1882, English naturalist.*

1242. **Some folks seem to have descended from the chimpanzee much later than others.**
—*Kin Hubbard*

1243. **One does not meet oneself until one catches the reflection from an eye other than human.**
—*Loren Eiseley*

1244. **In studying the traits and dispositions of the so-called lower animals, and contrasting them with man's, I find the result humiliating to me.**
—*Mark Twain [Samuel Longhorne Clemens, 1835-1910, U.S. author and humorist.].*

1245. **Darwinian man, though well behaved, At best is only a monkey shaved.**
—*W.S. Gilbert [of "Gilbert and Sullivan" fame, English musical composers.].*

※

1246. **If we look straight and deep into a chimpanzee's eyes, an intelligent self-assured personality looks back at us.**
If they are animals, what must we be?
—*Frans de Waal*

1247. **... the worst two she-devils in Chicago.**
—*noted Chicago newspaper publisher Joseph Medill, referring to his two daughters.*

1248. **I'm willing to die...but if I did, I'd take a thousand with me.**
—*Jim Jones, September 6, 1975, instigator of the infamous "Jonestown massacre" in Guyana, where close to one thousand innocent followers of the paranoid schizophrenic "Reverend" Jim Jones did perish, after being forced to drink cyanide-laced Kool-Aid.*

1249. **If you ever want to know the shape of your esophagus, breathe tear gas; you'll know the length, the width. The gas will immediately define it through its burning properties.**
—*Michelle Cabrera-Caruso, CNBC reporter who covered the riots in Athens, Greece. (Sarah Maslin Nir, <u>The New York Times</u>, Nov. 19, 2011, p. A15.).*

1250. **Inspiring. Holds out the possibility of a rational understanding of how to construct the good life with the aid of science, free from the accretions of religious superstition and cultural coercion.**
—*Financial Times, in a review of Sam Harris's "The Moral Landscape," <u>The New York Times Book Review</u>, Sept. 18, 2011, p. 4.*

1251. **Running for president is like sticking your face in the blade of a fan.**
—*Mike Huckabee, former Republican presidential contender in 2008.*

1252. **Hey man, same mud, same blood.**
—*Tony Mavroudis, an Army officer on a jungle patrol in Vietnam, when asked by a TV film crew about the relationship between his black soldiers and his white soldiers. (A few days later, he was killed by a booby trap.)*

1253. **'You ever been in a car crash? Done bumper cars? You know when that hit catches you off guard and jolts you, and you're like, what the hell? Football is like that. But 10 times worse. It's hell.'**
—*Kris Jenkins, a former NFL All-Pro defensive lineman. (<u>The New York Times</u>.)*

1254. **It would ... be a beautiful thing to pass through life together hypnotized in our dreams for your country; our dream for humanity; our dream for science.**
—*Pierre Curie, proposing to Manya "Marie" Sklodowska in 1894. (<u>Smithsonian</u>, October 2011, p. 84.)*

1255. **The air is precious to the red man, for all things share the same breath — the animals, the trees, the man. Like a man who has been dying for many days, a man in your city is numb to the stench.**
—*Chief Seattle (Sealth) – Suquamish.*

1256. **His sermon from the pulpit of that Harlem church rocked me ... He might be young – two years younger than I was – but he was fully loaded. He seemed unaffected by the crowd, at peace with himself. ... I was taken by his humility. It wasn't false humility; I knew the difference. Nor was it humility in the service of charm. This man was both determined to do what he saw as his mission – and truly overwhelmed by it. ... Here was the real deal, a leader both inspired and daunted by the burden he'd taken on. ... I said I'd help him any way I could. And for the next 12 years, that's what I did.**
—"MY SONG - A Memoir." by Harry Belafonte with Michael Shnayerson, Illustrated, 469 pp. Alfred A. Knopf. (Reviewed by Garrison Keillor, in The New York Times Book Review, Sunday, October 23, 2011, p. 15.)

1257. **That other book which I made before ... Maybe you remember it. But if you don't, it don't make no difference, because it ain't got nothing to do with this one.**
—"Mark Twain" [Samuel Longhorne Clemens, 1835-1910], in the first paragraph of his discarded sequel to "The Adventures of Huckleberry Finn."

※

1258. **When youthful and frisky, Albert Einstein would refer to himself as 'the valiant Swabian,' quoting the poem by Ludwig Uhlan: 'But the valiant Swabian is not afraid.'**
—John Updike, "Higher Gossip/Essays and Criticism," (Alfred A. Knopf, 501 pages.)

1259. **The two men had first met in 1869, after which Twain [Mark] noted that the newly elected president struck him as having 'the expression of a man who had not smiled for seven years, and who was not intending to smile for another seven.'**
—Allen Barra, "His last stand," a review of "Grant's Final Victory/Ulysses S. Grant's heroic last year," by Charles Bracelen Flood (Da Capo Press), in the San Francisco Chronicle and SFGate.com/Books/Sunday, December, 4, 2011, p. F5.

1260. **Our ape relatives enrich our lives on this wonderful planet. Their existence acts as a constant reminder to us that we humans are**

part of nature and not above it, that we are risen apes and not fallen angels.
—*Desmond Morris, "Planet Ape," Desmond Morris/with Steve Parker. Firefly Books Ltd. (G.B.) 2009. Published in the U.S. by Firefly Books (U.S.) Inc. Buffalo, NY. 288 pages.*

1261. **There are stars whose radiance is visible on Earth though they have long been extinct. There are people whose brilliance continues to light the world though they are no longer among the living. These lights are particularly bright when the night is dark. They light the way for mankind.**
—*Hannah Senesh, poet, playwright, and paratrooper (1921-1944).*

1262. **Wisdom begins in silence.**
—*the Talmud*

1263. **At some other point during my intermittently self-destructive existence, I heard someone's counselor say, "If it wasn't for drugs and alcohol, a lot of us would've killed ourselves."**
—*Carrie Fisher, "Shockaholic," Simon & Schuster, New York, NY, 2011, pp. 14-5.*

1264. **Better than the assent of the crowd:**
The dissent of one brave man!
—*Sima Quian (145-90 B.C.) "Records of the Grand Historian".*

1265. **Truth will set you free.**
—*Gospel according to John*

1266.

A. I ain't a Communist necessarily, but I been in the red all my life.
B. Anybody caught singing his songs without permission, Guthrie once advised, 'Will be mighty good friends of ours.'
C. Life has got a habit of not standing hitched. You got to ride it as you find it.
—*Woodrow Wilson "Woody" Guthrie, "seminal American folksinger," 1912-1967, <u>The New York Times</u> Editorial Page, January 2, 2012, p. A18.*

1267. **Teddy Roosevelt said, for example, that President Kinley had the 'backbone of a chocolate eclair' [an accent aigu/over the "e" in**

eclair], and that Thomas Jefferson and John Adams were as different as pickles and ice cream.'
—*The New York Times Book Review, citing the book "WORST OF FRIENDS/Thomas Jefferson, John Adams and the True Story of an American Feud." By Suzanne Tripp Jurmain. Illustrated by Larry Day. 32 pp. Dutton.*

1268. **Not everybody trusts a painting, but people believe photographs.**
—*Ansel Adams, 1902-1984, U.S. photographer.*

1269. **If it's not your cup of tea – Don't drink it!**
—*Courtesy of Christine O'Brien, speaking of not taking a job which is unsuitable for that particular person.*

1270. **I soon found out that I couldn't stand this woman.**
—*Edward Landberg, owner of the Berkeley Cinema Guild, commenting on his brief marriage to Pauline Kael, noted former theater critic for The New York Times. ("...locals grew accustomed to seeing her up on a ladder changing the Guild's marquee, a hip flask filled with Wild Turkey dangling from a belt loop."/The New York Times Book Review, Sunday, October 30, 2011., p. 13.)*

1271. **Your right to swing your fist ends where my nose begins.**
—*Andrew "Old Hickory" Jackson, 1767-1845, U.S. general, 7th president of the U.S. 1829-1837.*

1272. **At least once a week. I write down the epitaphs, I guess as a daily awareness of mortality that arms me against it. For instance: 'I knew this was going to happen.'**
—*Dustin Hoffman, U.S. actor, speaking of his "tombstone fantasies" indulged in weekly when he is depressed. (Giles Foden, The New York Times "Style" Magazine [NYTimes.com/Magazine], March 4, 2012, p. 103.)*

1273. **Sitting under high bookshelves stacked with classics, Hoffman offers his own explanation: "It's not intellectual. You're mostly aware of what you don't like. Henry Moore said something like that.**

   You keep chipping away at what isn't an elephant. And Miles Davis said: 'Don't play what's there, play what's not there' – I've put it on my wall. We think the conscious is the determining

factor, and actually it's the least reliable instrument. The knowing is the infringement. You find what is exposed."
—*Dustin Hoffman, U.S. actor. (Giles Foden, <u>The New York Times</u> "Style" Magazine [NYtimes.com/Magazine], March 4, 2012, pp. 102-3.)*

1274. **And just how long have we got the magic?**
—*Dustin Hoffman, U.S. actor and director, speaking of that last hour of light before it becomes too dark to continue with filming. (Giles Foden, <u>The New York Times</u> "Style" Magazine, NYTimes.com/Magazine], March 4, 2012, p. 101.)*

1275. **Partly Hoffman is running from the specter of depression: 'It's tactile, a green knot in my stomach,' he says.**
—*Dustin Hoffman, U.S. Actor, describing what his episodes of clinical depression feel like. (Giles Foden, <u>The New York Times</u> "Style" Magazine [NYTimes.com/Magazine], March 4, 2012, p. 102.)*

1276. **He was not of an age, but for all time!**
—*Ben Jonson, 1573?-1637, English playwright and poet: poet laureate 1619-37. [From his verses of praise, published in the Folio, ending with the above "celebrated encomium."]*

1277. **Benjamin Franklin, who founded the University of Pennsylvania, once defined true education as an 'inclination join'd with an Ability to serve Mankind, one's Country, Friends, and Family; which Ability ... should indeed be the great Aim and End of all Learning.'**
—*Benjamin Franklin [1706-1790] / Andrew DelBanco, <u>The New York Times</u>, Op-Ed, March 9, 2012, p. A21.*

1278. **Whosoever, in writing a modern history, shall follow Truth too near the heels, it may haply strike out his teeth.**
—*Sir Walter Raleigh, 1552?-1618, English explorer and writer, in his <u>History of The World</u>, written while imprisoned in the Tower of London, and later beheaded.*

1279. **My father moved lightly over the earth, scarcely leaving a footprint, scarcely a shadow.**
—*Michael Frayn, British playwright and novelist, from his book, <u>My Father's Fortune: A Life</u>.*

1280. **I have often quoted the advice that John Adams [1735-1826, 2nd president of the U.S] gave to a younger lawyer: 'Now to what higher object, to what greater character, can any mortal aspire than to be possessed of all this knowledge well digested, and ready at command to assist the feeble and friendless...?'**
—John Paul Stevens, retired U.S. Supreme Court Judge, The New York Review of Books, April 5, 2012, p. 56.

1281. **Love... is an ever-fixed mark,**
That looks on tempests and is never shaken; It is the star to every wandering bark.
—Shakespeare [1564-1616], Sonnet 116.

1282. **"... the closest thing to war you can get without an M-16 in your hand."**
—Clem Daniels, four-time A.F.L. All-Star running back for the Oakland Raiders, 1961-1967, describing the violence of professional football.

1283. **If the erect penis is not wholesome enough to go into museums, it should not be considered wholesome enough to go into women.**
—Anita Steckel, the "mission statement" for a group of like-minded female experimental artists known as the Fight Censorship Group. (The New York Times. Obituaries. March 27, 2012, p. A18.)

1284. **In 1924 Virginia ordered Ms. Buck [Carrie], 18 years old, un-married and pregnant, to be forcibly sterilized. Her legal guardian appealed, and the case made it to the Supreme Court. The winning argument blamed her pregnancy on hereditary weaknesses – in particular, her presumed feeble-mindedness. Justice Oliver Wendell Holmes Jr.'s majority opinion entered history. 'Three generations of imbeciles are enough.'**
—"Opinion," by Nell Irvin Painter (The author of "The History of White People"). "When Poverty Was White," the Sunday Review, The New York Times, March 25, 2012, p. 4.

❋

1285. **I wish to have no connection with any ship that does not sail fast, for I intend to go in harm's way.**
—Captain John Paul Jones, 1747-1792, American naval commander in the Revolutionary War, born in Scotland.

1286. **You may not be interested in war, but war is interested in you.**
—*Leon Trotsky, 1879-1940, Russian Communist revolutionary.*

1287. **"How Writing Is Written, ..."**
—*Gertrude Stein, 1874-1946, U.S author in France, from her book, Ida, Yale University Press.*

1288. **Poverty is the worst form of violence.**
—*Gandhi, Mohandas Karamchand ("Mahatma"), 1869-1948, Hindu religious leader, nationalist, and social reformer.*

1289.

A. Fortune scorns old age.
B. The power to please at first sight, which I had so long possessed in such measure, was beginning to fail me.
C. It was on that fatal day...that I began to die. [After he had been scorned by a 17-year-old London courtesan called La Charpillon, when he was in his 38th year.]
—*Casanova, Giovanni Jacopo, 1725-1798, Italian adventurer and writer.*

※

1290. **I love the freedom to roam the ocean and work for yourself.**
—*Bruce Shackler, 59, commercial fisherman, Kodiak, Alaska. (Parade magazine, April 15, 2012, p. 12.)*

1291. **If you can't feel sorry for yourself, you'll never be able to feel sorry for somebody else.**
—*Cartoon/Parade, April 15, 2012.*

1292. **Between the batteries [George] Mallory read Shakespeare and wrote letters home from a "mud hole crawling with rats" and rank with corpses. The war left a million British dead, and 2.5 million wounded. Bayonets, cavalry and trench warfare met up with new weaponry — machine guns, poison gas and air bombing. The result was gruesome: "Limbs severed by steel, skulls dripping with brain tissue, genitalia simply gone, displaced by a hole in the lower gut oozing intestines .... The smell in the trench was of fear, and of sweat, blood, vomit, excrement, cordite and the putrescence of cadavers." For the**

soldiers who survived "the war changed the very gestalt of death." Out of this came a toughened breed of climbers.
—Holly Morris, The Lure of Everest, in her review of "Into The Silence/ The Great War, Mallory, and the Conquest of Everest." By Wade Davis. Illustrated. 655 pp. Alfred A. Knopf. ("The New York times Book Review," Sunday, December 4, 2012, p. 14.)

1293. **Tibetans were similarly befuddled by the British Mission.**
   As one high lama reflected on the British endeavors in his spiritual autobiography: Some "left early to have limbs cut off, the others stubbornly continue to climb... I felt great compassion for them to suffer so much for such meaningless work." The Tibetans, it's worth noting, have no word for the summit of a mountain.
   —Ibid [93], p. 14.

1294. **Populations of all native Montana wildlife have been allowed to rebound except bison; it's time to take care of them like they once took care of us.**
   —Robert Magnam, 58, director of the Fort Peck Indian Reservation's Fish and Game department, who will oversee the transplanted Yellowstone bison program. (The New York Times, story by Nate Schweber, April 27, 2012, p. A11.)

1295. **No system of education known to man is capable of ruining everyone.**
   —Otto Neugebauer, "pioneering" historian of mathematics and astronomy in the ancient world.

1296. **The Caretaker is funny, up to a point. Beyond that point, it ceases to be funny, and it was because of that point that I wrote it.**
   —Harold Pinter, English playwright.

1297. **When you sleep in a house your thoughts are as high as the ceiling. When you sleep outside they are as high as the stars.**
   —an old Bedouin saying, courtesy of Ms. Toscane Clarey.

1298. **It's easy to believe in the separation of church and state when one has nothing but scorn for all organized religion. That was the position of Thomas Jefferson. Jefferson's hatred of the clergy and established churches knew no bounds. He thought** that members of the "priestcraft" were always in alliance with despots against liberty. "To effect this," he said—privately of course, not publicly—"they have perverted the purest religion ever preached to man, into mystery and jargon unintelligible to all mankind and therefore the safer engine for their purposes."

The trinity was nothing but "Abracadabra" and "hocus-pocus...so incomprehensible to the human mind that no candid man can say he has any idea of it." Ridicule, he said, was the only weapon to be used against it. It was thus no great task for him to urge, as he did in 1802, the building of "a wall of separation between church and state." As he provocatively declared in his "Notes on the State of Virginia", he was not injured by his neighbor's believing in twenty gods or no gad at all. "It neither picks my pocket nor breaks my leg."
—Gordon S. Wood, in his review of the book _Roger Williams and the Creation of the American Soul: Church, State, and the Birth of Liberty_, by John M. Barry. Viking. 464 pp. ("The New York Review of Books," May 10, 2012, p. 45.)

1299. **My business is to teach my aspirations to conform themselves to facts, not to try to make facts harmonize with my aspirations.**
—Noted British scientist and educator Thomas Henry Huxley, 1825-95, known as "Darwin's bulldog" for his advocacy of biological evolution.

1300. **Michael Fuller, the technician who built Crick and Watson's famous model of DNA, has seen 26 colleagues at Cambridge win Nobel Prizes over the past 58 years. The secret of their success? "Incredible egos. They just know, somehow, despite what anyone says, that they are right."**
—in a 2012 "New York Times Book Review" commentary on _Free Radicals_, a book about scientists by author Michael Brooks.

1301. **Far from being an abolitionist in 1958 Lincoln added that he had no doubt that slavery would be ended "in the best way for both races in God's own good time."**
—"The Collected Works of Abraham Lincoln," edited by Roy P. Basher (Rutgers University Press, 1953) Vol. 3, p. 181. [_The New York Review of Books_, June 21, 2012.]

1302. **Pettiness is pessimism's flower.**
—Frank Bruni, Op-Ed page, _The New York Times_, June 12, 2012.

1303. **Always try to associate yourself with and learn as much as you can from those who know more than you do, who do better than you, who see more clearly than you.**
—*Dwight David Eisenhower, 1890-1969, U.S. general: 34th president of the U.S. 1953-61; in his memoir At Ease.*

1304. **Do not try to do too much with your own hands...It is their war, and you are to help them, not to win it for them.**
—*advice on counter-insurgency by T.E. Lawrence (Lawrence of Arabia), 1888-1935, English soldier and writer.*

1305. **Thus play I in one person many people, / And none contented.**
—*William Shakespeare's "Richard II", fifth act.*

1306. **It's a vicious circle: despair leads people to self-medicate in ways that compound the despair.**
—*Nicholas D. Kristof, The New York Times, July 5, 2012, Op-Ed page.*

1307. **Everybody is a genius. But if you judge a fish by its ability to climb a tree, it will live its whole life believing it is stupid.**
—*Albert Einstein, 1879-1995.*

1308. **Yellowstone National Park may be the best place there is to reflect on the fact that we are all pond slime.**
—*Richard Fortey, Horseshoe Crabs and Velvet Worms/The Story of the Animals and Plants That Time Has Left Behind. (Alfred A. Knopf. Illustrated. 332 pp.*

1309. **A foolish consistency is the hobgoblin of little minds, adored by little statesmen and philosophers and divines. With consistency a great soul has simply nothing to do.**
—*Ralph Waldo Emerson (1803-1882), Essays: First Series. Self-Reliance.*

1310. **Rule number one in politics is: never invade Afghanistan.**
—*Reported to be Former British Prime Minister Sir Harold Macmillan's "favorite line".*

1311. **If you want to be happy for a moment, seek revenge.**
If you want to be happy forever, forgive.
—*the Dalai Lama*

1312. **Humanity needs to be reminded that the sun's putting out four hundred trillion watts every second of every day, and we should tap that.**
—*Danny Kennedy, one of the three founders of the residential solar-power company, Sungevity, in The New York Times Magazine, August 12, 2012, p.29.*

1313. **The willingness with which our young people are likely to serve in any war, no matter how justified, shall be directly proportional to how they perceive the veterans of earlier wars were treated and appreciated by their nation.**
—*George Washington, written in 1789. [Courtesy of Larry Ronan, M.D., Boston, August 13, 2012 – in the New York Times "To The Editor" section, August 20, 2012.]*

❋

1314. **As human beings are also animals, to manage one million animals gives me a headache.**
—*TERRY GOU, chairman of Foxconn, which has more than a million employees worldwide but is using a growing number of robots. [The New York Times "Quotation Of The Day" – Sunday, August 19, 2012.]*

1315. **Kindness is loving people more than they deserve.**
—*Joseph Joubert*

1316. **I don't understand what is really the big deal, but I understand that America is a puritan country and nudity is a big thing in America.**
—*An Israeli official commenting on the report that some U.S. Congressmen were criticized by fellow-members for having gone "skinny dipping" in the Sea of Galilee during an unofficial visit to the country.*

1317. **Standing on the Moon looking back at Earth – this lovely place you just came from – you see all the colours, and you know what they represent.**
 Having left the water planet, with all that water brings to the Earth in terms of colour and abundant life, the absence of water and atmosphere   on the desolate surface of the Moon gives rise to a stark contrast.
—*Buzz Aldrin, astronaut.*

1318. **Everything that used to be inside of him is now outside of him.**
—A New York city firefighter, responding to the 9/11 attack on the Twin Towers, describing the first body he had seen (most likely a "jumper") .

1319. **One walks on corpses, sits down to rest on corpses, one has one's meals on corpses. For about 10 kilometers there are two corpses of Fritzes [German soldiers] on each square meter.**
—A Red Army [Russian] soldier, writing to his mother in 1945. (The "New York Times Book Review," Sunday, Sept. 9, 2012, p. 10, quoting from the book The Second World War – By Anthony Beevor.)

1320. **What could be more beautiful that the heavens, which contain all beautiful things?**
—Nicolaus Copernicus (1473-1543), the Polish astronomer who first posited the heliocentric theory of our solar system.

1321. **Having shown that the [Edward] Teller scheme was a non-starter, [Stanislaw] Ulam produced, in his typically absent-minded fashion, a workable alternative. "I found him at home at noon staring intensely out of a window with a very strange expression on his face," Ulam's wife recalled. "I can never forget his faraway look as peering unseeing in the garden, he said in a thin voice—I can still hear it—'I found a way to make it work.'" [...] Late the next year [1952], "Ivy Mike" exploded in the South Pacific, and Elugelab island was removed from the map [by the first thermonuclear (hydrogen) device detonated by the U.S.].**
—from William Poundstone's review of the book, "Turing's Cathedral", by George Dyson. (The New York Times Book Review, Sunday, May 6, 2012.)

1322. **She was just an ordinary person, like us. Inside all of us, we can be saints. We just have to do the work. ["That's what Mother Marianne did," Liz Leyden, The New York Times]**
—CHARLOTTE RECARTE, on Mother Marianne Cope, who is to be canonized as a saint on Sunday [October 21, 2012, by Pope Benedict XVI]. (QUOTATION OF THE DAY, The New York Times, Oct. 17, 2012.) – "In 1883, she answered a call to help thousands of Hawaiians who were ill with a mysterious and disfiguring disease known as leprosy and who were being taken from their families and exiled to a remote peninsula on Molokai called Kalaupapa. / Would the nun take charge of the hospitals

and lead a ministry among these patients? / 'I am not afraid aft any disease,' she wrote, agreeing to what would become a more-than-30-year mission serving those banished to the towering sea cliffs of Kalaupapa." (Liz Leyden, <u>The New York Times</u>, Oct. 17, 2012.)

1323. **The life of the laws of war has not been logic. It has been experience.**
—Oliver Wendell Holmes Jr. 1841-1935, U.S. jurist.

1324. **"In Judaism, the health of the baby is more important than anything," Rabbi Golberg said. The harm, he added, would come if the baby was not circumcised. "A man who is not circumcised cannot understand the context of the Bible," he said. "It is very, very important."**
—Rabbi Goldberg, of the Bavarian city of Hof, Germany, in response to a German pediatricians' association, as well as a children's aid group, which were helping lead a petition drive calling for a two-year moratorium on the practice of infantile male circumcision in Germany. (<u>The New York Times</u>, Sept. 20, 2012, p. A6.)

1325. **In fact, the average life expectancy of an officer in a British bomb disposal unit at the time [London, 1940] was 10 weeks.**
—Elizabeth D. Samet, in her review of the book, "The Long Walk / A Story of War and the Life That Follows," <u>The New York Times Book Review</u>, Sunday, August 19, 2012, p. 13.)

1326. **I do not approve of public instruction in Sexual relations.**
When I teach my children to avoid the Devil I don't begin by giving them a letter of introduction to him and his crowd. I hope that a cure for syphilis will never be discovered. It is God's punishment for nastiness. Take it away and there will be more nastiness, and it will be necessary to
emasculate our children to keep them clean.
—Henry Eliot, father of the poet T.S. Eliot [The Waste Landl, in a letter to Henry's brother, Thomas Lamb Eliot, dated March 7, 1914. (<u>The New York Review of Books</u>, Oct. 25, 2012, p. 20.)

1327. **Everything should be made as simple as possible, but no simpler.**
—Albert Einstein, 1879-1955.

1328. **God had 'sent the calamity [of the Irish potato famine of the 1840's] to teach the Irish a lesson,' he declared, and 'it must not be too much mitigated.' Sometime later he wrote that the famine was a 'direct stroke of an all-wise Providence."**
—*Charles Edward Trevelyan, a British civil servant at the Treasury, who was in charge of much of the British response to the famine in Ireland. (Isaac Chotiner, in his review of John Kelly's book "Blighted / The Great Famine and the Saga of the Irish People". The New York Times Book Review. Sunday Oct. 14, 2012, p. 11.)*

1329. **If Beethoven were sent to nursery school today, they would medicate him, and he would be a postal clerk.**
—*Andrew Solomon, a lecturer in psychiatry at Cornell University, from his book, "Far From the Tree" – Scribner (publisher).*

1330. **Candy is Dandy but Liquor is Quicker.**
—*Ogden Nash*

1331. **Art is the lie that tells the truth.**
—*Pablo Picasso (1881-1973), Spanish painter and sculptor in France.*

1332. **I have it written in my will that my gravestone is going to say "Fun! Fun! Fun! Death." You should have fun throughout your life, with exclamation points, but in the end no matter what you do, you're going to die.**
—*Kara Swisher, "In Profile", San Francisco Chronicle, 5/29/12, p. 14.*

1333. **They happened to throw it where I was swinging.**
—*Gail Harris, the New York Giants first baseman, who hit two home runs and drove in seven runs on Sept. 21, 1967, against the Pittsburgh Pirates, leading the Giants to a 9-5 victory. (The New York Times, Obituaries, Nov. 23, 2012, p. B7.)*

1334. **If my name ever goes into history it will be for this act, and my whole soul is in it.**
—*Abraham Lincoln, commenting on his signing of the Emancipation Pro-clamation, on New Year's day, 1863.*

1335. **The run-up to the Iraq war also elicits one of the most pungent lines in the book. After Bush [George W.] told Jacques Chirac that biblical prophecies were being fulfilled and specifically that "Gog and Magog are at work in the Middle East," the French**

president decided, in Eichenwald's words, that "France was not going to fight a war based on an American president's interpretation of the Bible."
—*In the review of Kurt Eichenwald's book, "500 Days / Secrets and Lies in the Terror Wars." The New York Times Book Review. Sunday, October 7, 2012.*

1336. **The legendary Rabbi Hillel, of the first century B.C., told a would-be convert, in reply to the request to be taught all of the Torah while standing on one foot: "That which is despicable to you, do not do to your fellow. This is the whole Torah; and [the rest is commentary - ITALICS], go and learn it.**
—*Elizabeth Rosner, in her "San Francisco Chronicle and SFGate.com" Book Review, of Open Heart, by Elie Wiesel. Dec. 16, 2012, p. E5. [Unfortunately Rabbi Hillel would not have included the barbaric practice of male genital mutilation (circumcision) under the heading of "That which is despicable to you..." -- jmm.]*

1337. **It is indescribably beautiful.**
—*Yuri Gagarin, Soviet astronaut and the first man in space in 1961, describing the view from his space capsule of planet Earth.*

1338. **Ms. Marquez-Greene recalled that one day when she was a bit anxious, Ana turned to her and said, 'Don't let them suck your fun circuits dry, Mom.'**

     "This grief process is personal, it's long and it's complex, and it's different for every one of us," she said.

     She added, "But we're not going to let this suck our fun circuits dry."
—*Nelba Marquez-Greene, mother of Ana, 6, one of the 20 young students killed in the Newtown, CT, school-shooting tragedy. (The New York Times, Monday, January 21, 2013, cont. from Page A1.)*

1339. **[...] After overtaxing one of his informants, the shaman Dedeheiwa, about the reason for a succession of village fissions into smaller hostile groups, Dr. Chagnon found himself rebuked with the outburst, "Don't ask such stupid questions! Women! Women! Women! Women! Women!**
—*Nicholas Wade, in his review of the book "Noble Savages / My Life Among Two Dangerous Tribes - the Yanomamo and the Anthropologists", by [Dr.] Napoleon A. Chagnon. Simon & Schuster. 544 pages. (The New York Times, Tuesday, February 19, 2013, p. D3.)*

1340. **Or listen to Stanislaw Ochman, who transported the Jews of his village, Zdunska Wola, in Poland, in a wooden wagon to the cemetery where they were murdered. The children, holding their mothers' skirts, were often too short for the raked gunfire, and fell into the pit, still clinging, as soil was piled atop them. After the ditch was covered, he recalled, breathless with more than half a century of disbelief, 'the soil was still moving,' because, he said. 'they were still alive': 'The earth was moving!'**
—*Edward Rothstein, <u>The New York Times</u>, Friday, April 26, 2013, p. C32.*

1341. **The United States, as the black educator and writer W.E.B. Du Bois (1868-1963), had noted, referring to the importance of slavery to the nation's economic development, was 'built upon a groan.'**
—*In an essay from 'The Great Divide', at <nytimes.com/opinionator>.*

1342. **What people don't understand is that at the beginning you could get out. Everybody could get out. Nobody would let us in. Everyone could have been saved. Everyone.**
—*Henny Wenkart, in "50 Small Victories in a Time of Unbearable Loss", by Neil Genzlinger, <u>The New York Times</u>, Monday, April 8, 2013, p. C3.*

1343. **I've got maybe 10 years to ladle the butter into a jar for my kids and then die.**
—*Standup comedian Louis C.K., in his HBO comedy special "Oh My God".*

1344. **... thatt notheinge was spared to mainteyne Lyfe and to doe those things which seame incredible, as to digge upp deade corpes outt of graves and to eate them.**
—*George Percy, president of Jamestown, in a letter written in 1625 during the starvation period, (Nicholas Wade, "Girl's Bones Bear Signs of Cannibalism by Starving Virginia Colonists", <u>The New York Times</u>, May 2, 2013, p. A11.)*

1345. **And I'm very, very, very close to my mother.**
—*Corey Johnson, gay, HIV-positive, aspiring New York City politician. (Ginia Bellafante. <u>The New York Times</u>. May 5, 2013, p. 26.)*

1346. **Oh, Master, make me chaste and celibate -- but not yet.**
—*Augustine, A.D. 354-430, in his "Confessions".*

1347. **We love those who know the worst of us and don't their faces away.**
—*Walker Percy, Southern author and philosopher.*

1348. **We would like to say, 'Good night, Lee, rest in peace, our fallen soldier.'**
—*Ian Rigby, father of Lee Rigby, 25, of the Royal Fusiliers, who was hacked to death with meat cleavers on a street in London by two Muslim terrorists, having first been run over by their car. (John F. Burns, The New York Times, May 25, 2013, p. A8.)*

1349. **Hurricane Sandy left Meaghan B. Murphy and her husband, Patrick, without power for days; now their third child is due in July. "There was not much else to do," she said.**
—*The New York Times, May 27, 2013, p. A13.*

1350. **Old age is like trench warfare: you are fighting for your life every minute of the day and night.**
—*J. Michael Mahoney, writer and researcher.*

1351. **How can it be that mathematics, being after all a product of human thought independent of human experience, is so admirably appropriate to the objects of reality?**
—*Albert Einstein, 1879-1955.*

1352. **His "feelings...swelled within and came near stifling utterances" when he talked about slavery.**
—*William Herndon, Abraham Lincoln's law partner, commenting on Lincoln's passionate hatred of slavery.*

1353. **Who am I to judge?**
—*Pope Francis I.*

1354. **All the powers of earth seem rapidly combining against him. Mammon is after him; ambition follows, and philosophy follows, and the Theology of the day is fast joining the cry. They have him in his prison house; they have searched his person, and left no prying instrument with him. One after another they have closed the heavy iron doors upon him, and now they have him, as it were, bolted in with a lock of a hundred keys, which can never be unlocked without the concurrence of every key; the keys in the hands of a hundred different men, and they**

scattered to a hundred different and distant places; and they stand musing as to what invention, in all the dominions of mind and matter, can be produced to make the impossibility of his escape more complete than it is.
—*Abraham Lincoln* *

[*   "... The same is true of the 1857 Supreme Court decision in the case of Dred Scott, which declared that all black people were 'beings of an inferior order' who possessed 'no rights the white man was bound to respect' -- a judgment that provoked one of Lincoln's most passionate speeches, in which he spoke of the plight of anyone in America born black." (The New York Review of Books.)]

1355. **You cannot help but learn more as you take the world into your hands. Take it up reverently, for it is an old piece of clay, with millions of thumbprints on it.**
—*Writer John Updike, in a college commencement address.*

※

1356. **My books are water; those of the great geniuses are wine. Everybody drinks water.**
—*Mark Twain [Samuel Langhorne Clemens]*

1357. **A noisemaker's First Amendment right stops when a listener's Eighth Amendment right is impaired." / It's a city, not a cemetery. You can't tell everybody to go around wearing ear plugs."**
—*Henry J. Stern, who created the so-called quiet-zones when he was New York City's park commissioner. (Emily S. Rueb, The New York Times, July 13, 2013.)*

1358. **Let us pick up our books and our pens. They are our most powerful weapons. One child, one teacher, one book and one pen can change the world.**
—*Malala Yiusafzai, 16, who was shot in the head by the Taliban in Afghanistan in 2012 for attending school -- in a speech before the United Nations in New York. (Jennifer Preston, The New York Times, July 13, 2013, p. A4.)*

1359. **Williams [Mason B.], a historian specializing in urban politics, quotes Roosevelt [Franklin Delano] saying that La Guardia [Fiorello] "comes to Washington and tells me a sad story. The tears run down my cheeks and the tears run down his cheeks**

and the next thing I know, he has wangled another $50 million out of me."
—*"City of Ambition, FDR, La Guardia, and the Making of Modern New York", by Mason B. Williams, <u>The New York Times Book Review,</u> Edward Glaeser, Sunday, July 21, 2013, p. 16.*

1360. **Love! Love! Love! That is the soul of genius.**
—*Paul Rossi, New York, posted on "nytimes.com".*

1361. **I'd be a bum on the streets with a tin cup if the markets were always efficient.**
—*Warren Buffet, renowned American stock-market investor.*

1362. **How can it be that mathematics, being after all a product of human thought independent of human experience, is so admirably appropriate to the objects of reality?**
—*Albert Einstein, 1879-1955.*

❈

1363. **Care about what others think and you will always be their prisoner.**
—*Lao-tzu, 6th-century b.c. Chinese philosopher, reputed founder of Taoism.*

1364. **A noisemaker's First Amendment right stops when a listener's Eighth Amendment right is impaired." / It's a city, not a cemetery. You can't tell everybody to go around wearing ear plugs."**
—*Henry J. Stern, who created the so-called quiet-zones when he was New York City's park commissioner. (Emily S. Rueb, <u>The New York Times</u>, July 13, 2013.)*

1365. **In a letter to a fellow physicist in 1915, Albert Einstein described how a scientist gets things wrong:**
"1. The devil leads him by the nose with a false hypothesis. (For this he deserves our pity.)
"2. His arguments are erroneous and sloppy. (For this he deserves a beating.)"
According to his own rules, Einstein should have been pitied and beaten alike.

"Einstein himself certainly committed errors of both types," the astrophysicist Mario Livio writes in his enlightening new book, "Brilliant Blunders."
—*Carl Zimmer, "The Genius of Getting It Wrong", The New York Times Book Review, Sunday, June 9, 2013, p. 25.*

1366. **To err is human. To persist is diabolical.**
—*Seneca, Lucius Annaeus (c4 B.C. - 65 A.D.), Roman philosopher and playwright.*

1367. **What could be more beautiful than the heavens, which contain all beautiful things?**
—*Nicolaus Copernicus, 1473-1543, Polish Astronomer.*

1368. **A psychiatrist gives his patient a series of ink blots to analyse. The patient describes an erotic scene in each one. The psychiatrist tells him, "You seem to be preoccupied with sex." The patient protests, "You're the one with all the dirty pictures."**
—*SNN.*

1369. **"Pick up, Sweetie!" the desperate voice of a woman says. "I love you! ... There's a little problem."**

[In the new 9/11 Memorial Museum.] Some visitors gasp at the audio loops of final recorded messages from passengers realizing their jet was doomed.
—*Francis X. Clines, The New York Times, July 23, 2014, Editorial Page.*

1370. **I do not remember becoming old. All of a sudden, I was there.**
—*Elaine M. Brody, 1922-2014, The New York Times, William Yardley, July 20, 2014, Obituaries.*

1371. **" Fifty percent of my questions are about why their hair is not falling out. It is the zillionth time I have answered it. "**
—*Dr. Mahinder Watsa, 90, who writes the Ask the Sexpert column in a Mumbai newspaper, on Indian men who write in with unfounded fears about masturbation, The New York Times, QUOTATION OF THE DAY, August 8, 2014, p. A5.*

1372. **"What's the definition of a Jewish telegram? 'Start worrying. Details to follow.' "**
—*Old Jewish joke.*

1373. "... THE COURAGE OF GENIUS."

"*Doctor Zhivago* [by Boris Pasternak] will, I believe, come to stand as one of the great events in man's literary and moral history," wrote [Edmund] Wilson. "Nobody could have written it in a totalitarian state and turned it loose on the world who did not have the courage of genius."
—*Michael Scammell, "The CIA's 'Zhivago' ",* <u>*The New York Review of Books*</u>*, July 10, 2014, p. 41.*

1374. "There are two paths," he wrote. "The sages' religious-devotion, which is lovely because it overflows with the nectarous waters of the knowledge of truth," and "the lusty undertaking of touching with one's palm that hidden part in the firm laps of lovely-limbed women, loving women with great expanses of breasts and thighs.

"Tell us decisively which we ought to attend upon," he asks in the Shringarashataka. "The sloping sides of wilderness mountains? Or the buttocks of women abounding in passion?"
—*Bhartrihari, third century AD poet, as reported in* <u>*The New York Review of Books*</u>*, 6/26/2008, p. 34.*

Index of Quotation Numbers

A

B

C

E

H

L

M

N

Q

R

T

X

Y